The Prophetic Approach to FOCUS

Unearthing the Deep Mysteries of FOCUS

Dr. Margaret H. Moore

This book, or parts thereof, may not be reproduced in any form or by any means without written permission from the publisher, except brief passages for purpose of reviews.

Scriptures quotations are taken from many different translations noted on the reference page.

Library of Congress Number: 2017906079
Interior Illustration by Ms. Gabriel Crumpler
Publisher: Grace US Living Publications
Copyright © 2017 by Dr. Margaret H. Moore

ISBN: 978-0-692-11786-6

All rights reserved.

Printed in the United States of America

CONTENTS

Dedication
Foreword
Introduction...8

1st APPROACH ...10
Mind Penetration
Focused or Unfocused

2nd APPROACH...16
Mind Penetration
Permeates the Body

3rd APPROACH...27
Mind Permeation
Will Manifest

4th APPROACH...32
Mind Penetration
Psychological Battles and Body Response

5th APPROACH...45
Solutions to Strategies
that Render Us Unfocused

6th APPROACH...48
Becoming Unfocused Can Kill

7th APPROACH...75
David Is Forced by God to Refocus

8th APPROACH...98
The Woman at the Well
Made to Focus for the Other Side Ministry

9th APPROACH...119
Overflowing Joy X-Extreme Poverty
= A Well of Rich Generosity

10th APPROACH...146
An Uncontrolled Fire
Becomes a Controlled Fire

11th APPROACH...185
When There Is No King
In the Land

12th APPROACH...225
Another Gospel

Conclusion...252

About the Author
Let's Keep in Touch
References

DEDICATION

The Prophetic Approach to FOCUS is dedicated to all the upcoming mouthpieces of God. They are the ones that will understand the times and know just what God's people should do within those times.

(1 Chronicles 12:32)

FOREWORD

You may have already read, "There is a Call in the Land to FOCUS" by Melvin Moore. From that, you have learned the necessity to FOCUS or refocus your attention to the Word of God to escape the ills of society. In Margaret Moore's book, "A Prophetic Approach to FOCUS", you will discover great insights behind the attacks of Satan to steal, kill and even to destroy what God has for you. Satan uses distractions that rob you of focus, thereby robbing you of your purpose.

Man is a three part being spirit, soul (mind, will and emotions) and body. (I Thessalonians 5:24) You are spirit and soul that lives in a physical body. What you put in your soul affects your body. You may not have been aware of this truth in your life but "A Prophetic Approach to FOCUS" reveals these truths. We believe these truths will make you free. (John 8:32)

The world we live in has put man into slots to shape our thinking and behavior. The world tells us who we are and what we should do with our lives, and when our life is no longer useful. If you step outside of what man has define for you, then, you are considered rebellious, and a problem to society. All of the negative labeling and persecution has one goal in mind; it is to keep you in the slot, which the world has defined for you. We were created in the image and likeness of God. Jesus came to put you in a *mold*, not in a slot, so who He created you to be, will be seen. Proverbs 23:7 says, "As a man thinks in his heart, so is he."

"The Prophetic Approach to FOCUS" get right into the hearts of man. It exposes the heart that has shaped our thinking. You will read about our great heroes of faith like David, Paul, the Samaritan woman, Shunammite woman and many more. You will see the prophetic insight into their lives that looked like defeat but ultimately turned into great victory. "Above all, be careful what you think, because your thoughts control your life". (Proverbs 4:23 ERV) You will understand how their focus or lack thereof shaped their lives. You will understand how God's amazing Grace reshaped their lives, by refocusing them for success.

We believe as you read each encounter, you will see yourself and become more aware of how you think, and how your thinking has shaped your life. Get ready for God to refocus your life for great success!

Apostles Tony and Cynthia Brazelton

Introduction

The Prophetic Approach to FOCUS was written from a prophetic view. It prophetically speaks to the earth, calling her to give up God's sons and daughters that have prophetic voices and insight. These prophetic voices will unearth deep mysteries of God for the signs of the times. They will know precisely the prophetic words to release into the earth for that time. They will speak God's Word in truth to shatter the hard places in the lives of His people. They will prophetically place God's people into their prospective positions for ministry. Let them that have an hear, hear what the Spirit of God is saying to the church.

This book taps into the mysteries as in John 4. A woman sought to quench her thirst of loneliness, rejection, insecurity and love. Natural water did not quench her thirst. She simply needed a drink of Living Water to restore her focus. This book gives a prophetic approach into the lives of the Samaritan woman, David, Elijah, Shedrach, Meshach and Abednego, Isaiah and others. It explores the struggles they experienced to remain spiritually focused.

The sights and sounds from this physical world can become a distraction. It often takes us on a path, different from what God intended for our life. God is calling us to regain focus! His Word promised, "If we delight ourselves in the Lord, He gives us the desires of our heart", unearthed mysteries. God reminds us that our eyes have not seen, our ears have not heard, neither has it entered our heart the things God has for us. God wants us that have eyes to see, to see well. He wants us that have ears to hear, to hear well. God wants us that have a heart to understand, to understand well.

The Prophetic Approach to FOCUS will assist each person to examine themselves. Many that are thirsty, relentless and desire to unearth the mysteries of God will become focused. God desire for us to live life from His perspective. In doing this, we become focused and will develop a deeper commitment to Him.

Have you ever been distracted from carrying out what God called you to do? If so, from a prophetic approach, have a drink of the Living Water. If you drink the Living Water, you will never thirst again. *The Prophetic Approach to FOCUS* assist you to answer your call and to restore spiritual focus!

1st APPROACH

Mind Penetration
Focused or Unfocused

James 1:8 says, A doubled minded man is unstable in all his ways.

Let's approach focus by dealing with the flesh and the spirit. Whichever one we wax strong in, is the one we will obey. There is a war between the house of David (spirit) and the house of Saul (flesh). The house of Saul could not defeat the house of David. David's mind was on spiritual things and he cultivated them. Saul's mind was on natural things and he cultivated them. David rendered himself (mind), a servant to the spirit. Saul rendered himself (mind), a servant to the flesh. When we are unstable, we become divided in every area of our lives. The enemy seeks to make our mind unstable to prevent us from becoming effective for God. If he can convince us to accept what he presents as truth or fact, a battle begins in the mind. It will manifest itself to our body, making us ill. Once we become ill, our body or temple becomes paralyzed, rendering us useless to the kingdom. The Word says,

In the beginning was the Word and the Word was with God and the Word was God.   *(John 1:1) KJV*

The Word was the thought and mind of God. Before God created anything, He created it in His mind first. The mind is an important part of the body. It is the worst possible thing when our mind is under the attack of Satan. When Satan does not want us to be effective in the Kingdom of God, he will attack our mind. Attacks on the mind will cause us to give up. We may cease working with and for God. When we voice our tiredness, we are battling in our mind. Subsequently, if our mind has been transformed, we are equipped to deal with every situation in life.

The Word of God says that we are to serve God with our mind. Ultimately, Satan seeks to bind our minds to become unstable. He knows if the mind is loose, our body is loose. If our mind is in bondage, we are considered as brain dead. When we are brain dead, the body does not have the ability to move. We lack instructions and directions; therefore, we become paralyzed and immobile. We cannot speak because our mind has rendered the entire body as dead. Whatever is allowed to penetrate our mind will permeate our body.

If Satan can deceive us to accept what he presents as factual and truth, a battle begins in our mind. That battle will manifest from the mind to our body, and possibly cause sickness. If our mind has not been transformed, it could possibly limit our ability to perform activities of daily living. We cannot make sound decisions, think clearly and possibly lose our memory. When the enemy take control of our mind, our body will not function properly. Jesus declared in Matthew 8:20,

The foxes have holes, and the birds of the air have nests; but the Son of man hath not where to lay his head. (Matthew 8:20) KJV

Jesus is searching for a people or a body where He

can lay His head. We are Christ's body. We must give Christ a place upon His body to lay His Head. His Head upon His body gives us direction, authority, thoughts, ideas and the mind of Christ. Lazarus is a good example.

Let's imagine the process of Lazarus' mind when Jesus used the words "Lazarus comes forth"

The words traveled to Lazarus's mind, before his entire body moved. The mind must think and believe it can do something, before it does it. Jesus wept because the people in John 11 did not understand the day of their visitation. Jesus came to offer what the scripture declared, "Let this mind be in you that is also in Christ Jesus". He came so they would let His mind be in them. Jesus called Lazarus from the grave by his name. He could not call the body forth without calling his name. When Jesus called the name Lazarus, it registered in Lazarus' mind first, before the body moved. Lazarus' name is what Lazarus had in his mind. The body does not move unless the mind renders it to move. Jesus had to loose Lazarus' mind first. If Jesus had called Lazarus body first, he would have stayed bound. He would have remained in the grave. Jesus had to call his name because His name is what Lazarus knew in His mind.

Whenever there is an accident or injury involving an individual, the first question they are asked, "What is your name?" The question is asked because, if the name is not recognized, it could indicate something happened to the mind or head. Luke 8:26-36 says,

26So they arrived in the region of the Gerasenes, across the lake from Galilee. 27As Jesus was climbing out of the boat, a man who was possessed by demons came out to meet him. For a long time, he had been homeless and naked, living in the tombs outside the town. 28As soon as he saw Jesus, he shrieked and fell in front of him. Then he screamed, "Why are you interfering with me, Jesus, Son of the Most High God? Please, I beg you, don't torture me!" 29For Jesus had already commanded the evil spirit to come out of him. This spirit had often taken control of the man. Even when he was placed under guard and put in chains and shackles, he simply broke them and rushed out into the wilderness, completely under the demon's power. 30Jesus demanded, "What is your name? "Legion," he replied, for he was filled with many demons.

31The demons kept begging Jesus not to send them into the bottomless pit. 32There happened to be a large herd of pigs feeding on the hillside nearby, and the demons begged him to let them enter the pigs. So, Jesus gave them permission. 33Then the demons came out of the man and entered the pigs, and the entire herd plunged down the steep hillside into the lake and drowned. 34When the herdsmen saw it, they fled to the nearby town and the surrounding countryside, spreading the news as they ran. 35People rushed out to see what had happened. A crowd soon gathered around Jesus, and they saw the man who had been freed from the demons. He was sitting at Jesus' feet, fully clothed and perfectly sane, and they were all afraid. 36Then those who had seen what happened told the others how the demon-possessed man had been healed.
(Luke 8:26-36) NKJV

    This is a prime example of when the mind is distorted it can cause the body to function improperly. We can see that this man was in a mind, but it was not his right (transformed) mind. Satan feared that the man would become a powerful witness for God. Therefore, he attacked the man's mind. The man in the Gadarenes had a violation in his wonderful and fearfully made body. Satan convinced him to accept what he presented to him as factual and truth. The battle began in his mind and later manifested from his mind to his body. It made him sick psychologically and physically. Therefore, this rendered him ineffective and useless to the Kingdom of God.

According to the man's behavior, his mind needed transformation for a long time. He walked around naked and was driven into a place of isolation. In fact, he was homeless and lived in a community of dead people. His home was called tomb. Fetters and shackles restrained him. He had an evil spirit within him named "Legion". A "Legion" was at least six thousand demons. Sickness had violated his mind so deeply that he did not know his name. For example, when Jesus asked him his name, he said, "Legion". He called himself the name Satan wanted him to believe; "Legion". After Jesus, casted the demon out of the man, he was healed. He sat at Jesus' feet, fully clothed and perfectly sane.

Verse 36 says, "Then those who had seen what happened told the others how the demon-possessed man had been healed." This validates a fact that the sickness in his mind caused the entire body to not function properly. In other words, when the mind is the mind of Christ, the entire body functions effectively for the kingdom of God. The man became the witness for Jesus and Satan feared him.

Verse 35 states, "A crowd gathered around Jesus".

The man's ultimate purpose in the end was to become a vessel to gather crowds that would be attracted to Jesus. Our purpose is the same.

2nd APPROACH

Mind Penetration Permeates the Body

God desires us to focus our body and mind on wellness and healthy living. Divine healing is God's intention for us. Therefore, healing is a part of our inheritance of spiritual blessings, in heavenly places in Christ Jesus. It is a normalcy to be healed because it does not violate God's Word for good health. God designed all our body parts to work properly. This is God's intention: health and well-being for us. The Word of God says in Psalms 139:14, "I will praise thee, for I am fearfully and wonderfully made; marvelous are thou works, and that my soul knoweth right well." God blew the breath of life into us. We are made in the image of Christ. God did not design our body for sickness or corruption.

Romans 13:1 says, *"Let every soul be subject unto the higher powers. For there is no power but of God: the powers that be are ordained of God."* *(AKJV)*

When God's authority has been violated, it is a violation against God. We are created in God's image. He blew the breath of life into us. He said we were very good after He created us. Any other invasion violates our wonderful and fearfully made body. God placed an Immune System inside our body to automatically heal any injury or any type invasion that occurs without our permission. When David said, "We are fearfully and wonderfully made," he respected the detail of the anatomy and physiology of our body.

Integumentary System is the skin, which is the largest sensory organ of the body. It allows Vitamin D syntheses. It protects deeper tissues and organs. It regulates fluid and prevents massive blood loss.

Skeletal System is mainly the bones. It's calcium. It is the framework for the body. It protects vital organs. It also produces red blood cells.

Muscular System involves the muscles. They generate heat and use energy. Muscles create movement and maintain posture.

Lymphatic System contains lymph and lymph nodes. This system picks up fluids leaks from capillaries. It supports the immune system and houses white blood cells.

Cardiovascular (Circulatory) System consists of the heart. It permits blood to circulate. It transports nutrients, oxygen, carbon dioxide, hormones and blood cells. It stabilizes body temperature and Ph balance; maintaining homeostasis.

Urinary System contains the bladder and kidneys. It removes nitrogenous waste out of blood. It regulates electrolytes, fluid and pH balance.

Digestive System (Alimentary) is the mouth, throat, esophagus, stomach and intestines. It breaks food down into the building blocks for the body.

Respiratory System is the lungs, nose, mouth, pharynx, trachea, etc. It allows gas exchange system to rid the body of is carbon dioxide and take in oxygen.

Nervous System is a system in the body, which sends signals around the body.

Endocrine System secretes hormones that regulate growth, metabolism and general body function.

Reproductive System consists of the production of off- springs and hormones.

Immune System has portions of many different systems that fight disease.

LET US LOOK AT THE IMMUNE SYSTEM AND HOW IT WAR AGAINST SICKNESS

To be "immune" means to be protected. The immune system fights off sickness. It is the body's defense against infectious organisms and invaders. Through a series of steps called the immune response, the immune system attacks organisms and substances that invade or violate the body system to cause diseases.

Our skin protects our body from germs. When the skin is broken, even during surgery, germs can enter and cause infection. A wound is a break or opening in the skin. Wounds often occur because of an accident or injury. Types of wounds include: cuts, scrapes, puncture wounds, burns and pressure sores. A wound may be smooth or jagged. It may be near the surface of the skin or deeper. Deep wounds can affect: tendons, muscles, ligaments, nerves, blood vessels and bones. Minor wounds often heal easily, but all wounds need care to prevent infection. Wounds heal in stages. The smaller the wound, the quicker it heals. The larger or deeper the wound, the longer it takes to heal.

When you get a cut, scrape or puncture the wound will bleed. The blood will start to clot within a few minutes or less and stop the bleeding. The blood clots dries and forms a scab, which protects the tissue underneath from germs. Not all wounds bleed. For example, burns, some puncture wounds and pressure sores do not bleed. Once the scab forms, your body's immune system starts to protect the wound from infection. The wound becomes slightly swollen, red or pink and tender. You may see some clear fluid oozing from the wound. This fluid helps clean the area. Blood vessels open in the area, so blood can bring oxygen and nutrients to the wound. Oxygen is essential for healing. White blood cells help fight infection from germs and begin to repair the wound. This stage takes 2 to 5 days.

Tissue growth and rebuilding occurs next. Over the next three weeks or so, the body repairs broken blood vessels and new tissue grows. Red blood cells help create collagen, which are tough, white fibers that form the foundation for new tissue. The wound starts to fill in with new tissue, called granulation tissue. New skin begins to form over this tissue. As the wound heals, the edges pull inward, and the wound gets smaller. A scar forms and the wound becomes stronger.

As healing continues, the once affected area itches. After the scab falls off, the area may look stretched, red and shiny. The scar that forms will be smaller than the original wound. It will be less strong and less flexible than the surrounding skin. Over time, the scar will fade and may disappear completely. This process could take as long as two years. Some scars never completely go away. Scars form because the new tissue grows back differently than the original tissue. If you only injured the top layer of skin, you will probably not have a scar. With deeper wounds, you are more likely to have a scar.

For example, once I tried to cut the bushes outside of my house with the electric cutter. Just before I started, I had a vision that I would lacerate my finger with the electric cutter. Shortly after having the vision, I did just that. Soon after arriving to the emergency room, the physician stopped the bleeding, cleansed the laceration and placed stitches in my finger. I went to work the next day, despite needing the use my hands to work. I wasn't concerned; I knew in my mind that the healing process for my finger had begun.

The most uncomfortable part was the soreness. I knew eventually the cut would start to repair itself. I just went about my daily duties. There was nothing I could do but wait for the full manifestation of the healed finger. My body was well equipped with the natural healing process. Nothing extra was needed to speed up nor slow down the process. My body had the ability to reproduce a proliferation of new cells to replace the damaged cells. There was nothing I could do to produce new cells to replace the damaged cells. The healing happened involuntarily.

For example, despite our body functioning, our mind dictates if we feel sick. One day, I remembered arriving to work feeling perfectly fine. A colleague that I greeted each morning approached me. She asked, "How are you? You don't look too good." I assured her I was doing fine. She responded, "OH!" as if I was masking how I felt. I am the type person that is always optimistic and full of laughter. Soon after, another colleague began telling me how terrible I looked. After a while, the two interactions troubled my mind. I began to wonder about the spoken words that affected me mentally and physically from colleagues. I accepted what they stated, which was lies, as truth. It manifested itself into sickness. As a result, I believed I was sick. The reality was, as soon as I accepted their lie as truth, I became extremely sick with agitating flu-like symptoms: limp body, runny nose, headache, and cough. Bed-bound and medicine ready, I knew a visit to the doctor's office was inevitable.

Upon arrival, I found that every good doctor asks about your health history and listens to your self-prognosis. My physician confirmed, I was sick, based on everything I said. I felt sick. The more I imagined the sickness, while describing it, I began to feel worst. Now, the thought had even more validity, once the doctor said it. In my mind, if the doctor said it, it was so. The thought was embedded more in my mind, as fact and truth. Yeah! Now comes the rubber that meets the road. He wrote me a prescription. The prescription for medications validated that it was a legitimate illness. That made me accept it even more, as factual. Since I accepted the lie, my mind generated support and confirming thoughts of my illness. I did not challenge the thoughts.

Why should I challenge a thought that originated from me? The thoughts appeared to be my own, since they came from me. I believed me, therefore, I was more inclined to accept what Satan said to me. All I needed was to believe what I said to me as fact and truth. Whatever my mind accepts as truth influences my body. Satan wants us to believe and accept a lie. Satan does not care about us.

For As a man thinks in his heart so is he.
(Proverbs 23:7) NKJV

    Whatever is allowed to penetrate the mind as truth, will consume us. We act out what we count as truth. The same analogy goes; I allowed the thought of sickness to penetrate my mind first. Later my body took the penetrated thought of sickness from the mind, and it permeated my body. In the same vein; if I allowed my mind to become penetrated with thoughts of wellness and wholeness, it will permeate my body as well.

    According to the natural defenses in our body, there is power for healing. The first power for healing is built into the defenses God made when He created us. Next, we have extra power from the Holy Ghost to heal any type sin, sickness and disease physically or mentally. Physically, many sicknesses are eliminated when damaging emotions or stressors are eliminated. We can make ourselves sick with our emotions or stressors. Our mind can introduce damaging and harmful thoughts into our body. If these thoughts are accepted as truth and fact, we will allow sickness to overrule God's best, which is wholeness.

    Stress is our body's way of responding to a demand or threat. When we sense danger, real or imagined; the body's defenses kick into high gear in a rapid, automatic process called the "fight-or-flight" reaction or the stress response. The stress response is the body's way of protecting us. When our stress response works properly, it helps us stay focused, energetic and alert. In emergency situations, stress can save our life; giving us extra strength to defend ourselves. As an example, we are stimulated to slam on the brakes to avoid an accident. Stress can help us rise to meet challenges. Stress keeps us on our toes during work. It enhances our concentration when we attempt to win a challenge or drives us to study for an exam when we rather watch TV. Yet, beyond a certain point, stress stops being helpful. It starts to cause major damage to our health, our mood, our productivity, our relationships and our quality of life.

In a fight-or-flight response this is what happens in the body. When we feel threatened, our nervous system responds by releasing a flood of stress hormones, including adrenaline and cortisol. The hormones rouse the body for emergency action. The heart pounds faster, muscles tighten, blood pressure rises, breath quickens, and our senses become sharper. These physical changes increase our strength and stamina, speed our reaction time, and enhance our focus; preparing us to either fights or flight from the danger at hand.

The effect of chronic stress happens when our nervous system does not distinguish between emotional and physical threats. When we become super stressed over an argument, work deadline or bills; our body can react just as strongly as if we are facing a true life or death situation. The more our emergency stress system is activated, the easier it is to trip, and the harder it is to shut off. If we tend to stress frequently, our body may be in a heightened state of stress most of the time. That can lead to serious health problems. Chronic stress disrupts nearly every system in our body. It can suppress our immune system, upset the digestive and reproductive systems, increase risk of heart attack and stroke, as well as speed up the aging process. It can even rewire the brain, leaving us more vulnerable to anxiety, depression, and other mental health problems.

Health problems, exacerbated by stress includes depression, anxiety, sleep problems, eczema, weight issues, reproductive issues, memory and thinking problems and digestive problems. Signs and symptoms of stress overload, which is dangerous, can easily come upon us. We can get so use to stress overload, that it feels familiar and normal. We will not notice how much it affects us, even as it takes a heavy toll. Cognitive warning signs and symptoms of stress overload are memory problems, inability judgment, seeing only negative, constant worry, general unhappiness, agitation, moodiness, irritability, anger, feeling overwhelmed, loneliness, isolation and other mental and emotional problems. Physical warning signs and symptoms of stress overload are aches, pains, diarrhea, constipation, dizziness, chest pain, increased heart rate, libido and frequent colds or flu.

Behavioral warning signs and symptoms of stress overload are eating, little or too much sleep, withdrawing from people, procrastination, neglect responsibilities, use of alcohol, cigarettes or drugs to relax, nail biting, pacing floor or rocking. Causes of stress are related to situations and pressures that are called stressors. We think of stressors as being negative, an exhausting work schedule or a rocky relationship. Anything that place high demands on us can be stressful. Positive events as getting married, buying a house, going to college or receiving a promotion can be stressors. All stress is caused by external factors. Stress can also be internal or self-generated as we worry excessively about something that may or may not happen, or having irrational, pessimistic thoughts about life. What causes stress depends on our perception. Something that's stressful to us may not faze others; they may even enjoy it. A morning drive may make us anxious and tense; worrying about the traffic will make us late. Others may find the trip relaxing because they allow enough time. They enjoy music while driving.

Common external causes of stress are, major life changes, work, school, relationship issues, financial problems, being too busy, children family, etc. Common internal causes of stress are: pessimism, inability to accept uncertainty, rigid thinking, lack of flexibility, negative self-talk, and all or none attitude. Stressful life events according to Holmes and Rahe Stress Scale that contribute to illnesses are death of a spouse, close family member, marriage separation, imprisonment, injury, illness, marriage, retirement or job loss.

The widespread damage of stress differs from person to person. Some people can roll with life's punches, while others crumble into small obstacles or frustrations. Some people thrive on the excitement of a high-stress lifestyle. If we continue to punch a person in their arm with our fists, it may not hurt nor affect them in the beginning, but the more punches the arm receives, the more intense the pain becomes. The pain progresses slowly and possibly will have spasms. The process is the same when we continue to allow stressors to punch us day after day; eventually causing us to cave. When we counter attack Satan punches with God's Word, our body responds differently.

Casting down imaginations, and every high thing that exalteth itself against the knowledge of God, and bringing into captivity every thought to the obedience of Christ. (2 Corinthians 10:5) KJV

Finally, brethren, whatsoever things are true, whatsoever things are honest, whatsoever things are just, whatsoever things are pure, whatsoever things are lovely, whatsoever things are of good report; if there be any virtue, and if there be any praise, think on these things. (Philippians 4:7- 8) KJV

3rd APPROACH

Mind Permeation Will Manifest

We do not willingly come under Satan's influence. Satan's strategy is to render us ill through attacking our mind. He is relentless in trying to penetrate our thoughts with his ideas. If we are ignorant of his devices, we accept his ideas as fact. When we accept his ideas as fact the process starts. His ideas and thoughts, penetrates our mind, and prevent us from coping. The armor of God is designed to handle mental and spiritual attacks. It guards our mind from the enemy and rejects his thoughts and ideas. When we yield to him, he seeks to destroy us.

AN EXAMPLE OF A PREGNANT WOMAN

A false pregnancy is when a woman believes she is expecting a baby; when she is not. She may experience symptoms of pregnancy, but with the omission of an actual fetus. Doctors understand psychological factors can trick the body into thinking it is pregnant. This occurs sometimes when a woman feels an intense desire to become pregnant. Her intense desire may be due to infertility, multiple miscarriages, impending menopause or a desire to get married. Her body may produce many pregnancy signs. She may experience signs such as a swollen belly, enlarged and tender breast, nipple changes, possible milk production, feeling of fetal movement, interruption of the menstrual cycle, weight gain, nausea and vomiting. The brain misinterprets these signals as pregnancy. It triggers the release of hormones as estrogen and prolactin that lead to actual pregnancy symptoms. The woman's mind is signaling that she is pregnant and accepts it as fact. The body agrees with her mind, therefore responding and manifesting what the mind believes.

ANOTHER EXAMPLE

One woman's body literally responded to what was in her mind about getting pregnant every June. The stress of getting pregnant every June penetrated her mind so heavily; she thought she had become pregnant. Her menstrual cycle never came around in the month of June each year. Extreme fear of getting pregnant with twins again, penetrated her mind, her body responded to what her mind had accepted as factual and truth. The suggestion, idea and image as a fact in her mind, told her body it was so. Her body set out to get done what her mind said to do. The body accepted it as a fact and the signs and symptoms began to emerge.

 We can believe what we think is real, but it is only real in the mind. It is not real. Now Satan has something to work with. The idea planted in our mind does not have to be true. Satan knows how to time them, so we can accept them as our own idea or own thoughts. An idea or thought accepted as our own, even if false, damages the mind and body.

ANOTHER EXAMPLE

A mother may speak of being worried and sick over her daughter attending college away from home. This is the daughter's first year, and she has always depended upon the mother for everything. The mother is worried and sick. What if she gets caught up in peer pressure? There have been robberies on campus. What if she is robbed on campus? After all, there have been murders on campus. Now sick and worry is placed together as twins in her mind. Worry is a concern and agonizing over something that has not happened. This mother is stressing over something that has not happen yet. It does not have to be true at all. Worry is one of Satan's strategies of deception. The mind has a picture, idea or image of the worst. Since the mother was worried, deception paced in her mind all day. She tossed and turned all night without much sleep. Deception affected her body and manifested its symptoms. She could not drink or eat. Her heart was beating furiously, and stomach was upset. She could not think straight. All these symptoms were caused by what she saw, which really did not exist at all. Satan merely suggests or dropped an idea, image or picture into her mind.

Don't worry about anything; instead, pray about everything.
(Philippians 4:6) NLT

Tell God what you need and thank Him for all He has done. What we allow to penetrate our mind can leave us open to emotional assault. We have overcome many areas in our life, such as drugs, smoking, lying, stealing, drinking, fornication, adultery, cheating etc. Yet, it is hard for us to believe we can overcome emotional things as worry, fear, anxiety, as well. We are troubled on every side, over jobs, our children, neighbors, spouse etc. Some are disconcerted with any and everything. Some people manifest symptoms of sickness and diseases from being carriers of detrimental feelings.

We do not willfully place self under Satan's influence. Satan carries out his will in our lives through his many deceptions. He uses deception to encourage us to think what he desires us to think as being real. Once we believe him, we have swallowed his bait of deception. If we believe what Satan desire us to believe, it could have a profound effect upon our body, whether it is a lie or truth. The mind accepts these words as fact, and fact manifests into the body. Satan's focus is to exalt his knowledge in our mind (lies) and what he says over the knowledge of what God has said to us (truth)!

Another example

A woman decides to go to school. No matter how challenging it becomes, she is committed in her mind to having a perfect attendance. She was determined to keep these promises she made to herself. It did not matter if she felt tired, or symptoms of a cold or flu; she refused to submit to Satan's suggestions and ideas. She kept the promises she made to herself about attending school. Because of her decision, at graduation time she was in the top of her class. She had never become sick nor missed a day of school. She then realized, whatever she allowed to penetrate her mind would manifest into her body, if she accepted it as fact and truth. Therefore, she allowed wellness to penetrate her mind, and wellness manifested into her body. She accepted wellness fact and truth. She experienced manifestation of what her mind accepted as a fact and truth. What she allowed to penetrate her mind caused her body to respond. Her mind did the opposite of what her body was suggesting. She refused to allow the stressors of worry, anxiety thoughts, suggestions and ideas from Satan, dictate to her.

4th APPROACH

Mind Penetration
Psychological Battles and Body Response

Elijah is a mighty man of God. He allowed the suggestions, thoughts, images and ideas of Satan into his mind. He became focused on the words of Jezebel and accepted it as fact and truth. This made him sick emotionally. Fear penetrated his mind and caused a body response to unconsciously be set into motion. Whatever, can penetrate the mind, will cause a body response.

For as a man thinketh in his heart so is he. (Proverbs 23:7) KJV

    This scripture says, as a man allows thoughts, imaginations and ideas to penetrate his mind, so will his body response. There will be a manifestation of what he thinks. His body will respond to what he sees in his mind. Whatever a man focusses on in his heart, will appear. Satan uses deception to get into our mind. His goal is for us to receive and think thoughts from Him re real. He is persistent in persuading us to think these are our thoughts. He knows we are more likely to believe what he thinks is true. When we believe Satan's thoughts are our thoughts, we bite his bait of deception. If we believe what Satan says to us is factual and truth, it could affect our body. It does not matter whether it is true or not. If we believe it is as truth, our mind believes it as factual. We can believe what we think is real, but it is only real in our mind! It is not real at all.

Elijah had a psychological battle in his mind

The emotional stress from what Jezebel said to him manifested itself into his body. Fears from her death threat, made him flee into the wilderness. He became sick to the point, he became depressed. He ended up residing under a juniper tree and hibernated inside a dark cave. He felt alone, slept for days and wanted to die. He did not eat food nor drank water. He felt no one understood what he was going through. He acted as though what Jezebel said had happened. He went into complete isolation. Despite how he was feeling, we will see how God set in motion, healing for Elijah's mind, without Elijah's permission.

And Ahab told Jezebel all that Elijah had done and withal how he had slain all the prophets with the sword. (I Kings 19:1) KJV

    God raised him up to challenge Ahab and destroy the prophets of Baal. Ahab told Jezebel how Elijah wrought miracles. Elijah demonstrated great qualities in I Kings seventeen through nineteen chapters. He willingly placed his life on the line to prove Jehovah was God. After his prayers, the heavens were closed from rain for three years and six months. He outran Ahab's horses. He interceded to God to break three years of drought he had prophesied in the land. He challenged hundreds of prophets of Baal on Mt. Caramel. Fire came from heaven, consumed the sacrifice, trench of water, stones and dust of the altar. Afterwards, he killed all the prophets of Baal. Elijah challenged Israel to choose whom they would serve; God or Baal.

The showdown at Mt. Carmel proved that the prophets of Baal were impotent. All these things about Elijah caused the people to follow God. They were on Elijah's side because he showed how powerful God is. When Ahab told Jezebel how Elijah had executed all the prophets of Baal, which embarrassed her; she set out to kill Elijah.

Then Jezebel sent a messenger unto Elijah warning him that, so let the gods do to me and more also if I make not they life as the life of one of them (prophets that were dead) by tomorrow.
(I Kings 19:2) AKJV

Jezebel was angry about the death of the Baal prophets. She was furious that her supporters were eliminated, and felt her authority and pride were threatened. She seeks revenge of anyone who damaged her authority and pride. She hated when her followers died. The prophets of Baal were her support system. They prophesied only things she wanted to hear. They worshiped her and Ahab. Jezebel was wicked, evil and resentful. She devised plots to murder Elijah, based on what she heard about him. Jezebel prophesied to let the gods do to her and more, if Elijah was not put to death within twenty-four hours, just as one of her prophets were put to death. If Elijah remained on the scene, she could not continue her evil deeds. She swore by her gods to kill Elijah because she lacked control over him.

The spirit of Jezebel
Set out to kill God's prophet

She hated God's prophets because they set out to destroy altars she built for people to worship. They are called to destroy Jezebel and her followers. Satan plants Jezebel spirits in the land to try to penetrate the prophet's mind. Her (not a gender) job is to silence the voice of the prophetic word through the spirit of fear. She seeks control of prophetic authority through their thought life. She works strongly with demonic powers to deceive, defile and destroy God's rule. She used sexuality, seduction, manipulation, control, religion, fertility, perversion or multiplication of followers, like the prophets of Baal to war against others.

These spirits worked for Jezebel to build strongholds on people's mind. This spirit is like a virus that corrupts, distorts and reroutes all information about certain situations. It is like the HIV virus. The HIV virus also corrupts, distorts and reroute all information of the Immune System. The HIV virus permeates the body and changes itself to look like the helper cells in the Immune Systems. These disguised helper cells pretend to be cells that help the Immune System. This is symbolic of manipulative spirits pretending to help the immune system of the church. In its deception of pretense, this helper cell destroys every cell or member it contacts within the body. The main goal of the HIV virus and manipulative spirits are to control and eventually kill the body or person. This spirit is designed to shut down the person and anyone associated with the person. The goal is to destroy and disable individuals, ministries and churches. The longer this spirit operates within an individual, the harder it is for them to get delivered.

And when he saw that, he arose & went for his life & came to Beersheba, which belonged to Judah and left his servant there.
(I King 19:3) KJV

This was the beginning of Elijah allowing the thought, idea and suggestion of Satan, into his mind. He saw the image in his mind. When he saw it, he believed it, and accepted it as factual and truth. He began to manifest in his body what the mind accepted as factual and truth. He allowed the words and image to penetrate his mind. His mind could not handle all the stress. His mind manifested what it could not handle, to work with his hormones to secrete excessively.

THE *FIRST* PSYCHOLOGICAL BATTLE ELIJAH EXPERIENCED IN HIS MIND WAS *WORRY*

Worry caused the manifestation of anxiousness, torment, troubled and uneasy feelings about what was perceived as happening or could happen. He arose and ran for his life. He then went into…

THE *SECOND* PSYCHOLOGICAL BATTLE CALLED A *PANIC STATE*

A panic state manifests shortness of breath, increase heart rate, chest pain, increase respirations, trembling, fatigue, sweating, nausea, intense fear and impending doom. This great man of God feared no one the day before. Yet, the next day he was trembling before a woman from the kingdom of darkness. He was so intimidated by the thought, idea and image that penetrated his mind. It caused him to abandon the ministry God called him into. He was a man chosen by God into the prophetic office as a prophet. His confidence was broken down. Doubt and fear paralyzed him. A man who once was successful in ministry and moving is now immobilized.

The word of Jezebel plunged this mighty man of God from greatness to hopelessness and powerlessness. He took the idea, thoughts and image when he heard her words to kill him. Notice that Jezebel just spoke the words only. Neither action nor harm were inflicted yet. He allowed words spoken by a woman to penetrate his mind. Those very words controlled his life from that moment forward. His body responded to what he allowed to penetrate his mind. Fear consumed him. Earlier, this same man contended with Ahab, 450 prophets of Baal and faced all of Israel. Now, one spirit (Jezebel) terrified him.

4But, he himself went on a day's journey into the wilderness (desert) and came down and sat under a Juniper tree. He requested for himself that he might die. Enough, now O LORD, take away my life, for I am no better than my fathers.
5And as he lay and slept under a juniper tree behold, then an angel touched him and said unto him, arise and eat.

6And He looked and behold there was a cake baked on the coals and a cruse of water at his head, and laid him down again.

7 And the angel of the Lord came again unto him the second time and touched him and said unto him arise and eat because the journey is too great for the.
8 And he arose and eat and drink and went in the strength of that meat 40 days and forty nights unto Horeb the mount of God.
(I Kings 19:4-8) AKJV

Elijah went into the wilderness of Arabia, a desert place. He sat under a juniper tree to keep him safe from poisonous snakes, natural and spiritual. It is known that snakes will not go near this tree. Snakes are symbolic of the demonic forces that were not allowed to get to Elijah. The juniper tree served, as a hedge of protection. God placed it around him in the wilderness, following the images, ideas and thoughts that penetrated his mind. God led him to choose a tree that snakes were fearful of. People also used oil from this tree to anoint themselves. The oil is symbolic of the power of the Holy Ghost. Even in the times of Elijah, having an overwhelming cave mentality season, God kept his head anointed with oil.

This spirit of suggestion is so strong that it controlled the mind of this mighty man of God. His body responded to what his mind believed. He took the words, and ideas of Satan, into his mind. He accepted the words of Jezebel as factual and truth. Elijah had a psychological battle in his mind, which manifested itself into his body, urging him to quit and die. It made him sick mentally and physically, to the point that he was in a *flight*, but not a *fight* response.

THE *THIRD* PHYSIOLOGICAL BATTLE ELIJAH EXPERIENCED WAS *DEPRESSION*

He could not think but felt hopelessness and lost interest in daily activities. He was full of sadness and loss energy, which was a contributing factor to his immobility and paralysis. He refused to move and felt everyone was against him. In fact, he felt as though God had abandoned him as well. He felt all alone and self- pity. He would soon isolate himself in the darkness of a room known as a cave. He did not want to come out. No one understood what he was going through. He ate no food, drank no water and wanted to die. A spirit of assumption came upon him. He assumed his ministry was finished in the earth. Therefore, he desired to be released through death. He wanted to rid himself of the immediate trouble that plagued him. Elijah was not designed to die. That is why God did not respond to his request. He had been marked by God to be escorted to heaven in a whirlwind, according to scriptures;

And it came to pass, as they still went on, and talked, that, behold, there appeared a chariot of fire, and horses of fire, and parted them both asunder; and Elijah went up by a whirlwind into heaven.   *(II Kings 2:11) AKJV*

God did not grant his request to die; but made supernatural provisions to sustain and preserve Elijah's life. He gave him several prescriptions to heal his body and mind. He prescribed rest, food, water, exercise and to abide under the juniper tree. He knew Elijah was not in the right mind. Therefore, God took care of Elijah with supernatural provisions during his wilderness experience. God gave angels charge over him. He gave

Elijah the Bread of Life and Living Water(Himself). God is the Bread and God is the Water.

Therefore, when Elijah returned to ministry, he would be in the mind of Christ, and in the Power of Holy Ghost. God allowed him to sleep again to gain strength for a supernatural journey. He sent an angel to awaken the prophet to go to Horeb, the mountain of God. As Moses and Jesus fasted 40 days and nights, Elijah went in the strength of that same fast for forty days and nights.

9And he came thither unto a cave, and lodged there; and, behold, the word of the LORD came to him, and he said unto him, what doest thou here, Elijah? 10And he said I have been very jealous for the LORD God of hosts: for the children of Israel have forsaken thy covenant, thrown down thine altars, and slain thy prophets with the sword; and I, even I only, am left; and they seek my life, to take it away.

11And he said, Go forth, and stand upon the mount before the LORD. And, behold, the LORD passed by, and a great and strong wind rent the mountains, and brake in pieces the rocks before the LORD; but the LORD was not in the wind: and after the wind an earthquake; but the LORD was not in the earthquake: 12And after the earthquake a fire; but the LORD was not in the fire: and after the fire a still small voice.
(I Kings 19:9-12) AKJV

After going in the strength of supernatural meat for forty days and nights, Elijah went into a cave to lodge or live there. This is symbolic of a cave mentality. The mind of Elijah was in such a desolate state. It was because he accepted the ideas and thoughts of Satan as factual and truth. Even God asked him what were his reasons for being there. God wanted to know why he accepted the ideas and thoughts of Satan. God was saying, "Elijah why did you go there with Satan? No, you didn't go there; really?"

Why was he in that state of mind? God knew Elijah accepting the suggestion of Satan, was out of character for Elijah. Elijah went on a tantrum of what he accepts as fact in his mind. He believed these things were true because it fit his culture at that moment! He proclaimed to God he had been zealous in serving Him. He declared himself as the only prophet left because God's other prophets were killed. Now they are trying to kill him. He went on to accuse Israel of breaking covenant with God. He reminded God how he tore down the prophets of Baal altars. Elijah spoke out of the deception that had griped his mind.

His cave mentality launched him into this isolated spirit. The Word says, we have passions like Elijah. This tells me as he suffered, complained, isolated himself and prayed passionately so shall we. We like Elijah, will be harassed by Satan to manipulate and control our mind, if we accept his ideas and thoughts as factual. God had to deal with the suggestions, ideas and images Satan penetrated in Elijah's mind as factual. He had to replace the thought, image, and idea that caused him to become unfocused. God had to penetrate the world Elijah found himself in. He lived in a world in the futility of his mind suggested by Satan. Mind suggestions are so powerful that we unconsciously yawn if someone else yawns.

God had to call Elijah to come out of what he became use to, during this wilderness period. The trial period had engulfed his life and became his culture. He had received and became use to the culture of Satan dictating to his mind. In that cave mentality were lingering spirits of isolation, self-pity, depression, etc. These spirits wanted Elijah to stay inside that dark area and continue to minister to his mind.

God allowed the noisy elements to manifest so Elijah could see the type of nature raging in his mind and body. These temperaments reflected the emotional roller coaster feelings of Elijah. Elijah's moods reflect that of a storm. These emotions became what I would call, "Elijah's stormy self." One moment he was like the wind, the next he was like the earthquake, and then fire. God brought them to the forefront, so he could see it was all self (flesh) and not God. God brought Elijah out of the cave, so he could see "SELF". He wanted him to see the darkness of the cave. God is Light; therefore, when Elijah comes out into the light, he walked into the Light. The more Light he walks into, the more he sees the culture of the cave. The more Light he walk into, the more he will be able to identify lingering spirits out to control him.

The noisy elements (stormy self) were speaking to him very loudly, sounded like clanging cymbals. The noisy elements purposely spoke loudly. Their purpose was designed to drown out the voice of God. They caused all types of destruction. The earthquake's sound and temperament, rumbled to shake things up. The fire's temperament intent was to burn things up and destroy communities. The fierce wind temperament is that of a hurricane destroyer.

All noisy elements are symbolic of stormy tribulations and trials that believers may encounter during ministry preparation. God must reveal to us the difference between His voice and another voice. As sheep, we are to hear the LORD's voice. Satan disguises himself as an angel of light. He parades himself in a magnified way, in an attempt to convince us that what he is telling us is from God.

The still small voice of God, finally penetrated the mind and spirit of Elijah. It is the only voice that counts. God's voice brings a sense of stillness! The noisy elements of wind, earthquake and fire do not bring a sense of stillness. His still small voice will demand that peace must be still. Who could ever think that peace needs to be still; only God?

13And it was so when Elijah heard it, that he wrapped his face in his mantle and behold a voice unto him and said what dost thou her Elijah.
14And he said, I have been very jealous for the Lord God of hosts: because the children of Israel have forsaken thy covenant, thrown down thine altars, and slain thy prophets with the sword; and I, even I only, am left; and they seek my life, to take it away.

> *15 And the Lord said unto him, Go, return on thy way to the wilderness of Damascus: and when thou comest, anoint Hazael to be king over Syria: (I Kings 19:13-15) AKJV*

Through reverence, Elijah perceived God's presence. He wrapped his face during the *still voice*. Notice he did not wrap his face during all the *noisy elements*. It was because the presence of God was there. God is in the *Still Small Voice*. Elijah had been used to the Presence of and recognized it. Elijah came out of the cave to hear God, and to enjoy the Presence. He came out from among that culture to hear God.

God told Elijah to go and do something because he is still called as God's prophet. His current life's circumstances did not disqualify him from moving in ministry. God gave him instructions and directions to anoint three different people. He had to anoint Hazael as king of Syria and Jehu as king over Israel. The very last and important thing God told Elijah to do was to anoint Elisha to be a prophet in his room. God never addressed the things Elijah went on a tantrum about at his pity party. God never addressed the things he complained about at his pity party. God did not deal with the carnal things, but he did address Elijah's concern about the prophets. He basically said, "if I took care of you Elijah while you were not in your right mind and unfocused, surely, I can take care of my other prophets. God said to his great minister of God, "I have preserved 7000 other prophets in Israel who never bowed or kissed Baal."

5th APPROACH

Solutions to Strategies That Render Us Unfocused

4For the weapons of our warfare are not carnal but mighty in God for pulling down strongholds, 5casting down arguments and every high thing that exalts itself against the knowledge of God, bringing every thought into captivity to the obedience of Christ.6And having in a readiness to revenge all disobedience, when your obedience is fulfilled.   (II Corinthians 10:4-6) NKJV

We live in this world, but we refuse to do what the people of the world do. Women and men of God realize the battles we encounter daily are spiritual. Spiritual weapons are necessary to counter Satan's strategies and deception against our mind. Faith in God and prayers, as well as obedience to the Word of God, are very effective weapons. As Paul can see himself as a warrior warring against the proud logic in his mind, we too have the same ability. Paul was willing to become focus on God.

THE NATURAL MIND ALLOWS THOUGHTS, IDEAS AND IMAGES TO ARGUE AGAINST THE TRUTH

It is best described as rising above the knowledge of God. We must cease from allowing Satan's information to rise above what we know God has said to us in His Word. When God exposes a promise to us from the Word, Satan blocks of deception comes immediately, to steal that seed or Word. He tries to replace it with a lie. Therefore, we are to bring all the thoughts captive, that Satan parades before us and render them useless. When we do this, we destroy all types of pride that prevents us from knowing God. Pride, in our acquired worldly knowledge, has no room for God. We must commit to signing a peace treaty in our mind. A commitment contract will bring all ideas, thoughts, images and ideas in obedience or in prison to obey Christ. Making that commitment keeps our focus on Christ. Scriptures says,

7 And the peace of God, which surpasses all understanding, will guard your hearts and minds through Christ Jesus.
8 Finally, brethren, whatsoever things are true, whatsoever things are honest, whatsoever things are just, whatsoever things are pure, whatsoever things are lovely, whatsoever things are of good report; if there be any virtue, and if there be any praise, think on these things.   (Philippians 4: 7-8) NKJV

In verse 7, it says that the peace of God will guard or place a fortress around our hearts and mind through Christ Jesus. The peace of God is holiness that floods our soul, when we lean hard upon God. His peace stabilizes us throughout life. Peace is medication that overrides all nervousness, anxiety, and fear; along with psychological and physical sickness.

The scriptures give advice on the purpose of the mind. We are in control of our thought life, and what we focus on. Our focus lies in positive thinking and believing the Word of God. The Word says, 'It is impossible to entertain bitter and sweet water at the same time". We cannot entertain good and evil thoughts at the same time. Whenever a thought, idea or image comes to us from Satan, we should get rid of it quickly. We do this by meditating on the words of Christ. There is danger in allowing Satan to entice us to think negatively. It will lead to becoming unfocused. These scriptures in of Philippians 4: 7-8, gives a clear description of the attributes about Jesus. When we focus on and think about, what He thinks about, we become focus. God is true. He is honest. He is just. He is pure. He is lovely. He is of a good report. He is virtue (of moral excellence). He is praise worthy.

6th APPROACH

Becoming Unfocused Can Kill

The sin of disobedience caused David to become unfocused. Sin lurks when we neglect what God calls us to do. Without realizing, David was in more danger in Jerusalem, than if he had been out on the battlefield with his men. In other words, David laid aside his armor of God and surrendered to his wandering eye. Lust took over.

And it came to pass, after the year was expired, at the time when kings go forth to battle, that David sent Joab, and his servants with him, and all Israel; and they destroyed the children of Ammon, and besieged Rabbah. But David tarried still at Jerusalem.   II Samuel 11:1) AKJV

It was springtime, David stayed home from war against the Ammonite. Spring was the best time for kings to go into battle. During this time, they were assured of good weather and food. The roads were dry, and made traveling much easier to move supplies, chariots and troops. Instead of going to war, David chose to send Joab and his servants. They destroyed the Ammonites and surrounded Rabbah. Their fortification put an end to the Ammonites power and made them subjected to Israel.

In 2 Samuel 10, Joab and the army of the mighty men were preserved against the Syrians and the Ammonites, but they did not win an important victory. The important victory came when David led the battle at the end of II Samuel 10. Through custom and experience God communicates to David, "You need to be at the battle". In Galatians 5:16 there is a standard that speaks out loud and clear a profound truth:

This I say, walk in the Spirit, and ye shall not fulfill the lust of the flesh.   Galatians 5:16) AKJV

If David had his FOCUS where God wanted it, he would never have placed his focus, where God did not want it. He would have heard God's voice clearly and moved beyond what his flesh dictated. While Joab was busy laying a fortification for Rabbah, Satan was busy laying a fortification for David.

Satan has intention of entangling David into a web of distraction

Once David is entangled in that web of distraction, Satan will cause David to see more than he intends to see. Satan will take him farther than he intends to go. Satan will have him to do more than he intends to do. We will soon see David's lack of focus on God will cause him to fall deeper and deeper into the grip, control and clutch of strong deception. As David starts his downward spiral, he will become more unfocused. The upcoming episode with a woman will make it appear, David never knew God. David's behavior will resemble those in the world that live according to the world's standards. The god of this world blinded his mind.

David will proceed in walking out lust of the eye, lust of the flesh and pride of life. It is difficult to believe that this mighty man of God, whom loved God with all his heart, soul, mind and body, will lose his spiritual mind. The compilation of the web of distraction will be many. He will abandon his focus and purpose, by staying home from war. Instead, he will focus on his own desires, and not God's. He will deliberately sin by embracing temptation, instead of fleeing it. He intentionally will do wrong, though he knew what is right. He will cover his sin, deception, and murder a man. David will have a choice to stop and turn from evil on his road to distraction. Sin's characterization is to take control and rule his body. It is difficult to stop sin once the body yields to obey Satan. It is much easier to stop a tractor-trailer when it is on the top of a mountain, than when it is halfway down the mountain.

Then it happened one evening that David arose from his bed and walked on the roof of the king's house. And from the roof he saw a woman bathing and the woman was very beautiful to behold.
(II Samuel 11:2) NKJV

Apparently, David had too little time on his hand. If he had been at war, he would have plenty to keep him busy. Instead, David lusts after something God forbids.

LET US VISIT THE PERSONIFICATION OF SIN

The manifestation of sin began to move into its perfect work. Evening or darkness is a sign or indication that the SUN or SON has gone down. The kingdom of darkness increases demonic activity in the evening or when the SUN goes down. Whatever light or relationship David had with God, the SUN (SON) was about to go down.

But unto you that fear My name shall the Sun of Righteousness arise with healing in His wings. And ye shall go forth grow up as calves of the stall.   *(Malachi 4:2) KJV*

When Jesus, the light of our life, is hidden or obliterated by darkness, it is said the SUN (SON) is gone down. David arose from his bed and walked on top of the roof. Did he have trouble falling asleep or staying asleep? Did he suffer with insomnia or uneasiness? Did these things linger because he was not focused on God's will? While not serving in war where God wanted him, he was idle, not working and doing nothing. His idleness is an advantage given to Satan.

For we hear that there are some which walk among you in a disorderly, working not at all, but are busybodies.
                         (II Thessalonians 3:11) KJV

In the meantime, Bathsheba was at her house in a closed courtyard. She was very beautiful to focus upon.

Her beauty made the scenery even more tempting. She was extremely alluring in her facial and body features. David looked out and *saw* a naked woman bathing. At that very moment he *saw* her, he conceived the seed of sin. In other words, the moment he saw her beauty and nakedness, he imagined, considered, and visualized what he desired. At that moment, in his mind, he became naked. Mentally, his clothes were already off, and David casted off righteousness.

It was evening; around the time most people were asleep. Did Bathsheba consciously, know her bath and body was visible from the roof? Could she subconsciously desire her body to be an impressive view for a king? In the end, no matter her heart motive or intent, it was still no excuse for David's sin. His sin was not in seeing Bathsheba. I do not believe David said in his mind, "Let me go out and see if a woman is naked and bathing on her rooftop tonight". David's motives could have been pure, when he went outside. David's sin was in choosing to continue to focus his eyes on the appealing image after he saw what he saw.

The potency and force of temptation lies deep within the heart of the one being tempted. Satan strategically arranged for David to take a fall. But the Word says, God would give David a way to escape the temptation. This temptation was not too strong for David to escape, no matter how beautiful Bathsheba was. For example, Joseph was tempted more severely to commit sexual sin than David, but fled temptation.

There hath no temptation taken you but such as is common to man: but God is faithful, who will not suffer you to be tempted above that ye are able; but will with the temptation also make a way to escape, that ye may be able to bear it.
(I Corinthians 10:13) AKJV

David saw Bathsheba and her body as beautiful, but never thought how God saw him. Call it what God calls it – sin! Society calls it an affair, but God calls it adultery.

27Ye have heard that it was said by them of old time, Thou shalt not commit adultery: 28But I say unto you, That whosoever looketh on a woman to lust after her hath committed adultery with her already in his heart. 29And if thy right eye offend thee, pluck it out, and cast it from thee: for it is profitable for thee that one of thy members should perish, and not that thy whole body should be cast into hell.   (Matthew 5:27-29) AKJV

Jesus is saying, the real problem is in the heart. Looking at a person for arousing illicit sexual desires is adultery within the heart. Looking is feeding the eye to become unfocused. The eye is the inlet and outlet of wickedness. A "look" is unsafe and damaging to the one that is looking. It is better to lose the eye that offends, than to give in to sin. God requires an operation upon the eye if it lusts. God said, "If thy right eye offends thee or cause us to offend by looking or desiring; just pluck it out. If there is no way to restrain us, it is best to get rid of that eye. It is beneficial that only one member (eye) should perish; rather, the whole body to be cast into hell." Jesus is saying that we must deal drastically with sin, so we can refocus. A person is tempted to do wrong when he allows his bad thoughts to dictate to him. When he moves out and does what the bad thoughts tells him to do; he sins. When sin completes its work, it brings death.

14 But each one is tempted when he is drawn away by his own desires and enticed. 15 Then, when desire has conceived, it gives birth to sin; and sin, when it is full-grown, brings forth death. (James 1:14-15) NKJV

LET US EXAMINE THESE SCRIPTURES

But every man is tempted (lured) when he is drawn away of his own lust (desire) and enticed (seduced). When lust hath conceived (lust has a womb), it bringeth forth sin (sin is the child's name), and sin, when it is full grown (sin has to grow up), when it is finished, (sin has work to do and to finish), bringeth forth death (sin's mission in life is to be a murderer).

The source of David's temptation stemmed from being drawn or lured away due to his own lust and desire for someone. Let us personify this passage of scripture. The Word said, "When lust conceives, it will bring forth sin." This tells us that for anything to conceive, it must have a womb. Conception happens within the womb. It is the beginning of a new life. Scripture said, "when" lust conceives; not "if" it conceives. The scripture maintains, once lust conceived, it brings forth sin. At the appointed time for birth, whatever was conceived within the womb came forth or out. In this case, Sin was birth, brought forth or came out. The scripture also gives a name to the thing birthed out of lust's womb. Sin is the name given. We see that Sin is said to become full grown. For something to become full grown it must go through growth stages. Sin's journey went from infancy, childhood, adolescence and adulthood or full-grown.

The scripture says, "When sin is full grown it bring forth death". Most full-grown people have work, or an occupation they must perform. Sin's job or occupation when full-grown is to deliver or bring death to as many as it can. Sin was born to grow up to become a murderer. When we see the Word "bring", it means we can expect a transport of something. In this case, Sin transports death. Sin impacted a lot of people and covered large areas because death is a destiny assignment.

Lust drew David away from his position. His position should have been in fellowship with the Word of God and spiritual things. Instead, lust enticed, lured and seduced him. Lust hypnotized him and placed a stronghold upon him to prevent his escape. When David surrendered to his desire, he joined himself to a guilty union. The two became one flesh. Sin had work to do, and a job to finish in David.

Let Us Visit Another Analogy Of Sin

Sin pulls us away, like a fish being lured to bite a hook.

As the fish is lured, enticed and follows his bait, he is being taken to his death. Instead of the fish receiving a meal, he becomes a meal. The trap led him to his death. Ultimately, sin separates us from God. When sin is finished, it gives us a paycheck. The wages of sin is death.

A little leaven leavens the whole lump. (Galatians 5:9) NKJV

A little yeast permeates the entire loaf of bread.

The process of sin begins in our members or in our body. It begins as a small amount, but the small amount of leaven, can leaven the whole loaf. A small amount of yeast causes the entire loaf of bread to rise or swell. The yeast permeated the entire loaf and changed the whole structure of the dough. A little amount of sin permeates the entire body and can change its whole structure.

Once upon a time, there were a man well known who held an official office. His entire body structure was permeated and changed. He was tempted by his own desires for another woman outside of his wife. Those desires lured and seduced him away from his position as spouse, father and official. He later joined himself to the other woman. Sin permeated his entire body. He left his wife and children. We can say that sin changed his DNA. After Sin finished him, she brought forth death to him and his family. Sin permeated his entire body to murder him. The wages of sin is death, according to the Word. He lost his family, career and his name.

HERE ARE OTHER EXAMPLES TO VISUALIZE HOW EASILY SIN CAN PERMEATE THE BODY

One roach in a house can permeate an entire house with roaches. We can think there is one roach in the house, until the lights are out. Immediately, after the light is turned on, many roaches will run, scatter and hide. Whenever any type food is cooking in the kitchen, the smell permeates the house. This smell does not remain in the kitchen only; it spreads throughout the entire house. It is the same analogy with sin. Just as these examples can permeate entire areas, so it is with a little unchecked sin. Sin permeates the entire body.

Bathsheba was the leavening (swelling) of the whole loaf or body for David. The desire to sin began to rise within David. That is why Jesus said, "If your eye offends, pluck it out." Therefore, staying home from war provided the avenue or seed within him. The lack of focus caused the leaven to rise or to manifest. It appeared that David had been with several concubines and wives for at least the past twenty years. Apparently, his many wives did not satisfy his lust. It could have been that, David did not want Bathsheba, but was not satisfied with what God had given him. This proves true, the sins of the father visit the sons. This is exemplified in the life of David's son; Solomon. Solomon had 700 wives and 300 concubines. David and Solomon both proved if one woman is not enough, 5000 women are not enough.

> *So David sent and inquired about the woman. And someone said, "Is this not Bathsheba, the daughter of Eliam, the wife of Uriah the Hittite?"*   II Samuel 11:3) NKJV

This was the hot pursuit of his desire. He played it in his mind. Someone told David the woman's identity. "This is Bathsheba, the daughter of Eliam-one of David's Mighty Men at war. Her grandfather is Ahithophel, one of David's chief counselors. This is the wife of Uriah, the Hittite. The statement that "this is the wife of Uriah, the Hittite, lets us know, David learned Bathsheba was married. She was the wife of one of his mighty men. The woman came from a notable and upper-class family. Despite, who she was, her married status rendered her off-limits. Discovering her identity should have been a warning for the king. Since David learned her husband was at war, did this make the situation far more tempting? Did he assume it would be easier to get away with it? No matter the reason, David committed adultery in his heart first. Now he has an opportunity to commit adultery in action. Adultery is now in both his heart and mind.

David saw a beautiful naked woman. He saw (1) the beautiful (2) the naked and (3) the woman. This is the 3-fold ministry of Satan to steal, kill and destroy David. After seeing the beautiful, the naked and the woman, David was filled with lust. He entertained the temptation, instead of fleeing. What he focused on became a permanent snapshot in his mind. The longer he focused on that snapshot of the beautiful, the naked, and the woman, the more intense his desire became. At this stage, we see David, a great conqueror, now being conquered. This mighty man of God is led into captivity by his own lust. David was caught in this sin because he neglected his business. He should have been at war. If David had been in position, he would have been focused.

And David sent messengers and took her; and she came in unto him, and he lay with her; for she was purified from her uncleanness: and she returned unto her house.
(II Samuel 11:4) KJV

David's affair with Bathsheba was not the beginning of his chain of events from adultery to murder. He showed his disregard to God's plan for marriage years before. David's life always consisted of having more than one wife, according to I Samuel 25. His reputation of adding more wives showed lack of restraint. This is a corrupted seed sown long ago. It grew unchecked and continued to bear bitter fruit. Proverbs 23:7 says, *"Whatever a man thinketh in his heart so is he."* Whatever men focus on within the heart, that thing will consume them. Without a vision or focus on God, a man will perish or cast-off restraint. When the restraints were cast off, the eye was filled with trash, lust and distractions.

David inquired about Bathsheba. The corrupt desire within David grew more violently, even after knowing she was a married. Despite knowing, he sent the messengers for her. He used his power and authority God gave him as king, to take advantage of another man's wife. David, a man after God's own heart ignored every way of escape God presented to him. Notice how Bathsheba did not hesitate but came at his request. Of course, she is not completely free from blame, but offered no resistance. After all, there is no evidence of her being taken by neither force nor reluctance. Could it be she consented because David was great and famous?

When she arrived, David laid with her. In other words, he had intercourse with Bathsheba. Apparently, David's many wives and concubines were not enough. Neither did he consider Uriah as his loyal man; he totally disrespected him. Bathsheba was a lady of a good reputation, before David sent for and corrupted her. He ruined his life and the lives of many others, due to his lack of focus. The ultimate blame is placed upon King David. He knew his act was wrong, yet he did it. The cost of the payment for this sin was greater than pleasure. The wages of sin is death. Death can be seen in many faucets for him.

The cost of his sin would result in:
- Murder
- An endless threat in his family
- Family rebellion
- Others will sleep with his wives
- Unwanted pregnancy
- Murder of a trusted friend

- A dead baby
- Daughter Tamar raped by his son, Amnon
- One son murdered by another son
- A civil war by one of his sons
- A son imitating David's lack of self-control that leads Israel away from God.

What? Know ye not that he who is joined to a harlot is one body with her? "For two," saith He, "shall be one flesh."
(1 Corinthians 6:16) AKJV

Don't you know that when you give yourselves to obey someone you become that person's slave? If you are slaves of sin, then you will die. But if you are slaves who obey God, then you will live a godly life.

DAVID BECAME A SLAVE TO SIN

He joined himself to sin. He was controlled and obeyed his master of sin. To flee this type temptation and remain focus, we must submit to God, resist the devil and he will flee.

And the woman conceived; so she sent & told David, and said, "I am with child." *(II Samuel 11:5) NKJV*

Bathsheba was apprehensive about the outcome. Therefore, she told David about the pregnancy. Her message to David was an appeal for the king to take the necessary steps to prevent the penalties of their sin. Leviticus 20 states that both persons in an adulterous relationship are put to death. Bathsheba's situation was risky because everyone knew her husband was at war. David and Bathsheba did not plan this. The fruit or leaven of sin brought about the fruit of a child. They were terrified because the *problem* of pregnancy meant the adultery would be found out. The pregnancy created complications for David because Uriah was away at war. Therefore, Uriah could not be the father of the child. The hidden works of the Satan is revealed due to David becoming unfocused. Just as our first parents, Adam and Eve sought to cover their sins, so did they. His deceptions led him into a web of distractions to cover his sin. David, the adulterer, became a liar, a schemer and a murderer. David's life is out of control because he became unfocused.

6 David then got in touch with Joab: Send Uriah the Hittite to me." Joab sent him. 7When he arrived, David asked him for news from the front—how things were going with Joab and the troops and with the fighting. 8And David said to Uriah, Go down to thy house, and wash thy feet. After Uriah left the palace, an informant of the king was sent after him.

9But Uriah didn't go home. He slept that night at the palace entrance, along with the king's servants. 10David was told that Uriah had not gone home. He asked Uriah, "Didn't you just come off a hard trip? So why didn't you go home?" 11Uriah

replied to David, "The Chest" (heart) is out there with the fighting men of Israel and Judah—in tents. My master Joab and his servants are roughing it out in the fields. So, how can I go home and eat and drink and enjoy my wife? On your life, I'll not do it!"
(II Samuel 11:6-11) MSG

Uriah, the Hittite was one of David's mighty men. He and fellow soldiers were risking their lives in war for David. Yet, David used his authority to take advantage of Uriah's wife, and she became pregnant. After hearing this news, David moved into a strong spirit of deception. His first attempt was to cover up the pregnancy, by calling Uriah home from battle. David got in touch with Joab, the captain of the army. He commanded him to send Uriah home without revealing the reason to him.

When David heard the disastrous news of Bathsheba's pregnancy, he should have repented. Instead, he did what most sinners do; hide his sin. Sin is a barrier to our spiritual life and can hinder our fellowship with God. David's plan of deception was to avoid taking responsibility. He made small talk and questioned how things were going on the battlefield with Joab and the troops. Usually a messenger would have this privilege of carrying this information to the king.

ANOTHER PLAN OF DAVID'S DECEPTION

Uriah should go and sleep with his own wife. He believed if Uriah had intercourse with her while home, his sin would be covered. Bringing him back home will produce a great reason for her pregnancy. Therefore, the child that is already conceived would be passed off as Uriah's, child. The phrase "wash thy feet," suggests the agenda of relaxing at Uriah's house. Therefore, Bathsheba could plan an intimate evening with him. David contributed by sending the finest food and drink to help entice an intimate evening. However, Uriah refused! He was an honorable and faithful man. Uriah dare not think about enjoyment of the comforts of home, while his fellow soldiers were on the battlefield. Instead, he ended up sleeping at the palace entrance with the king's servants.

David disappointed, questioned Uriah about his refusal to go home, as the king had instructed. Uriah answered David, as a true soldier would. "With Israel army at war with the enemy, I refused to leave the battlefield to enjoy the comforts of home." He was a team player. He did not want to enjoy any comforts, while his fellow soldiers endured the hardship of war. Uriah showed himself to be more righteous than David.

On the other hand, David neglected his duty. He stole the wife of his best soldier. He committed the sin, while others placed their lives on the line for the king. David hoped Uriah proved to be like himself. He assumed Uriah would abandon his men for pleasure. Instead, Uriah proved to be a man of integrity.

12And David said to Uriah, "Tarry here today also, and tomorrow I will let thee depart." So Uriah abode in Jerusalem that day, and the morrow. 13 And when David had called him, he did eat and drink before him; and he made him drunk: and at evening he went out to lie on his bed with the servants of his lord again but went not down to his house.   (II Samuel 11:12-13) KJV

    David persisted in his deception to cover up his sin. He lied to Uriah, knowing that he wanted to get back to the battlefield with his soldiers as soon as possible. Yet, David delayed Uriah's return to war for two days, to devise another plan of deception. He hoped Uriah would treat this evening as his last before returning to battle. First, David attempted to break Uriah's reasoning by giving him too much to drink. He called Uriah to eat and drink with him. He hoped to get Uriah drunk to weaken his determination to be with his fellow soldiers. David efforts succeeded in getting Uriah drunk. Yet Uriah did not go home to Bathsheba. Instead, Uriah again slept at the palace entrance with the king's servants. He refused to enjoy the comforts of home, and his soldiers could not.

    There are differences in Uriah drunkenness and David drunkenness. Uriah became drunk with wine when he consumed it. David was drunk with lust when he slept with Uriah's wife. He hoped Uriah's drunkenness would bring the same result he experienced; intimacy with Bathsheba. Uriah's focus superseded the effects of alcohol. It did not soften Uriah's determination to remain a man of integrity.

    Could it be that Uriah suspected unfaithfulness in

Bathsheba and avoided her? Could he smell the scent of sin? Sin has an odor. In his effort to remain loyal Uriah was drunk in the spirit, while David was drunk with wine in excess. Being drunk with wine in excess or drunk with sin, changed David into another man. He was made drunk in excess from the lust of flesh, lust of eye and pride of life. He used and abused his God given authority and position.

14In the morning David wrote a letter to Joab and sent it with Uriah. 15In the letter he wrote, "Put Uriah in the front lines where the fighting is the fiercest. Then pull back and leave him exposed so that he's sure to be killed." 16 So Joab, holding the city under siege, put Uriah in a place where he knew there were fierce enemy fighters. 17 When the city's defenders came out to fight Joab, some of David's soldiers were killed, including Uriah the Hittite.
(II Samuel 11:14-17) MSG

David became more unfocused and more desperate to cover his sin. He was caught in a web of distraction. When David failed in covering up his sin, through the previous plans of deception, he began to plot his loyal soldier's death. He decided to send orders to the battlefield for Joab, the commander of the army. He would tell Joab to set Uriah in the forefront of the hottest battle. For the plot to be successful, Joab had to withdraw the other soldiers, so Uriah would be left alone. This strategy would ensure Uriah's death in battle. David wrote a letter for Uriah to deliver to Joab. Uriah's own hands delivered a letter to Joab with premeditated orders for his own death. David's deceit set up this most self-sacrificing man, to be the carrier of orders. The orders detailed the way he was to be murdered. David trusted the integrity of Uriah so much; he made him the unsuspecting messenger of his own death sentence. He was confident in Uriah's loyalty that he dare not peek. Satan planted the seed in David's heart to kill Uriah.

The dangers of war would be David's method to kill an innocent man

David, entangled in the web, had no thought of God's righteousness while Uriah was consumed with righteousness. When the next battle happened, Joab executed the orders of King David. Failing in past attempt to cover his sin, David wanted Uriah dead. Uriah had the most dangerous post assigned to him. It was strange that Joab would carry out such a plan from a letter, without knowing the reason. Joab probably wondered what Uriah had done to deserve death, but he obeyed King David's orders. He knew it was wrong, but simply followed orders, and allowed Uriah's to be murdered. Uriah's death was hidden by war, but his murder was just as though David had killed him. David became a murderer. If a child was to be born, Uriah's lips will not be able to disown it.

    David showed more integrity, while a servant, than a king. As a servant, he feared to touch God's anointed. It is the sole reason he did not kill Saul, his adversary. Yet, as king, he murdered his most faithful soldier.

David hid, and indulged in his lusts for years. His temptation turned into lust, and his lust turned into adultery. When the disadvantages of his adultery threatened to expose his sin; he covered it, first with deception and then with murder. Satan never tempted David all at once.

DECEPTION TOOK DAVID THROUGH THE PROCESS OF SIN TO BECOMING FOCUSED

18Joab sent David a full report of the battle. 19He told the messenger, "Tell the king everything that happened in the battle. When you are finished, 20his anger might explode. He might ask you, 'Why did you go so close to the city to fight against it? Didn't you know that the enemy soldiers would shoot arrows down from the wall? 21Don't you remember how Abimelek, the son of Jerub-Besheth, was killed? A woman dropped a large millstone on him from the wall. That's how he died in Thebez. So why did you go so close to the wall?' If the king asks you that, tell him, 'And your servant Uriah, the Hittite, is also dead.' 22The messenger started out for Jerusalem. When he arrived there, he told David everything Joab had sent him to say.

23The messenger said to David, "The men in the city were more powerful than we were. They came out to fight against us in the open. But we drove them back to the entrance of the city gate. 24Then those who were armed with bows shot arrows at us from the wall. Some of your special troops were killed. Your servant Uriah, the Hittite, is also dead." 25David told the messenger,

"Tell Joab, don't get upset over what happened. Swords kill one person as well as another. So keep on attacking the city. Destroy it.' Tell that to Joab. It will cheer him up."
(I Samuel 11:18-25) NIRV

    Joab sent a full report to David of everything that happened in the battle. The most important point in the report was music to his ears, "Uriah the Hittite is also dead"! Joab knew David was an experienced military man. He may have responded angrily if he heard a bad report on what he considered foolish military tactics. The idea about Abimelech in verse 21 was that he was too close to the wall and was killed in battle. Joab knew getting to close to the walls was a bad military move. Therefore, Joab performed the bad military move upon David's command. This maneuver endangered more soldiers and resulted in greater loss of lives. The move of killing other soldiers ensured Uriah would die as well. This strategy was like infecting the lives of a small sampling of young men with an infection and possibly killing them. A greater good would come out of it. Many were saved through learning about this infectious disease. The greater good in this small sampling of men targeted to die, would not implicate David as Uriah's killer.

    The messenger did not wait for the king's reply to share the news of Uriah's death. "Uriah the Hittite is dead also." These words had music David longed to dance to. The words rendered relief and secret satisfaction. His mission was complete. Uriah, the Hittite was dead. David could now marry Bathsheba and have a legitimate explanation for her pregnancy. "The sword devours one, as well as another". This was a proverb regarding fortunes of war. When becoming unfocused causes, you to kill, the conscience is seared. Therefore, David was saying, "these things happen". David said it to his own guilty conscience as much as he said it to Joab. David's response to Uriah's death was insensitive. Why? He had become callous in his own sin and heart. David's first act of sin led him to sin repeatedly, until he no longer felt guilty.

THE LONGER WE SIN, THE EASIER IT BECOMES TO REPEAT IT

His conscious had been seared, as with a hot iron. Strikingly, Uriah was a good man with strong spiritual character. How is it that David grieved deeply for Saul and Abner, his rivals, but showed no grief for Uriah? Sin trapped him into a web of distraction!

26And when the wife of Uriah heard that Uriah her husband was dead, she mourned for her husband. 27 And when the mourning was past, David sent & fetched her to his house, & she became his wife, & bare him a son. But the thing that David had done displeased the LORD.   (II Samuel 11:26-27) KJV

This text describes Bathsheba as Uriah's wife and not

by her name. It is intentionally done to accent David's sin. In bible times, death was usually mourned for seven days. When Bathsheba mourned her husband's death she wore mourner's clothes, weeping and sat in dirt. She also covered her head with dirt and ashes. Could she have known David arranged her husband's death and concealed all from her? Could she have been relieved to hear of her husband's death? If relieved at least she would escape the wrath and danger of being punished as an adulteress. The reward for her, from this ordeal is she would become queen.

David continued to work his plan of deception. Shortly after Uriah's death, David took Bathsheba as his wife. He took her to his house and she bore a son. This disrespectful act was nothing new for David. His life consisted of adding wives. He simply added another. In the eyes of the people, David marrying Bathsheba made him look like a hero. The people noticed how he cared for the poor, pregnant wife and the widow of one of his fallen captains. Many saw David as honorable. His acts seem that he was showing honor for his soldiers. They admire him for taking care of their widows when they are killed in battle. They marveled, "What a marvelous king!" Yet, we see God displeasure with David becoming unfocused.

27And when the mourning was past, David sent and fetched her to his house, and she became his wife, and bare him a son. But the thing that David had done displeased the Lord.
(II Samuel 11:27) AKJV

Though David could conceal his sin from people, God knew about it all. Eventually, he will become focused and submit to God's discipline in days ahead. David's sin will not go unpunished. The scheme of deception worked from the human point of view, but not from God's point of view. God sits high and look low. The adultery, lies, deceitfulness, murder and the marriage, displeased God.

God is not a God that has pleasure in wickedness. The Lord examines the righteous, but hates wicked and those who love violence.   *(Psalms 11:5) KJV*

David was under intense conviction and the joy in his life, evaporated. He had stress and agony that comes from living a double and false lifestyle. David lived in a place of having too much sin in him, to be happy in God, but had too much God in him, to be happy in sin. It was nearly impossible for him to be happy in God. He found no relief until he repented to God about becoming unfocused. Becoming unfocused will blind the eye, sear the conscience and confuse our entire spiritual nature, as with David.

Despite David's sin,
He was a man after God's heart

God drew David to repentance and restoration. He understood God was a God of mercy and lovingkindness. Psalms 51 is explicit on how terrible David felt, separated from God by way of sin.

1Have mercy upon me, O God, according to thy lovingkindness: according unto the multitude of thy tender mercies blot out my transgressions. 2Wash me throughly from mine iniquity, and cleanse me from my sin. 3For I acknowledge my transgressions: and my sin is ever before me. 4Against thee, thee only, have I sinned, and done this evil in thy sight: that thou mightest be justified when thou speakest, and be clear when thou judgest. 5Behold, I was shapen in iniquity; and in sin did my mother conceive me.

6Behold, thou desirest truth in the inward parts: and in the hidden part thou shalt make me to know wisdom. 7Purge me with hyssop, and I shall be clean: wash me, and I shall be whiter than snow. 8Make me to hear joy and gladness; that the bones which thou hast broken may rejoice. 9Hide thy face from my sins, and blot out all mine iniquities. 10Create in me a clean heart, O God; and renew a right spirit within me.

11Cast me not away from thy presence; and take not thy holy spirit from me. 12Restore unto me the joy of thy salvation; and uphold me with thy free spirit. 13Then will I teach transgressors thy ways; and sinners shall be converted unto thee. 14Deliver me from blood guiltiness, O God, thou God of my salvation: and my tongue shall sing aloud of thy righteousness. 15 O Lord, open thou my lips; and my mouth shall shew forth thy praise.

16For thou desirest not sacrifice; else would I give it: thou delightest not in burnt offering. 17The sacrifices of God are a broken spirit:

a broken and a contrite heart, O God, thou wilt not despise. 18Do good in thy good pleasure unto Zion: build thou the walls of Jerusalem. 19Then shalt thou be pleased with the sacrifices of righteousness, with burnt offering and whole burnt offering: then shall they offer bullocks upon thine altar.

(Psalms 51) KJV

7th APPROACH

David Is Forced by God to Refocus

After David's plot of the murder of Uriah, he kept up his public and private duties every day. It was his policy to keep up his good appearance in the government and public worship. Outwardly, David passed as a good ruler and man of example. He conducted himself as though he had not sinned. Man looks at the outward appearance, but God looks at the heart.

1And the Lord sent Nathan unto David. And he came unto him, and said unto him, there were two men in one city; the one rich, and the other poor. 2The rich man had exceeding many flocks seven herds: 3But the poor man had nothing, save one little ewe lamb, which he had bought and nourished up: and it grew up together with him, and with his children; it did eat of his own meat, and drank of his own cup and lay in his bosom and was unto him as a daughter. 4And there came a traveller unto the rich man, and he spared to take of his own flock and of his own herd, to dress for the wayfaring man that was come unto him; but took the poor man's lamb and dressed it for the man that was come to him.
(2 Samuel 12:1-4) AKJV

The other life David lived was a life of a man that sinned against God. Inwardly, he lived a lie. He had a seared conscience and dull in hearing God's voice. He was double minded, with a cold and hard heart. David had a form of godliness and denied the power thereof. He held the truth of God in unrighteousness. David's sin displeased the Lord. Despite, David's lack of hearing God, God's mercy and grace continued to follow him. Therefore, God had to send a man called Nathan to speak to him directly.

Nathan was a gift from God

He was God's representative and spokesman, full of wisdom. Therefore, he was called to tear down this altar that God did not build. Nathan assumed the role of a prophet, friend, counselor and personal advisor to the king. He was honorable and had great influence. The Word of the LORD was in his mouth. He was willing to speak the truth, even when he knew it would cause pain and discomfort. At this moment Nathan's office is higher than the king's office. The prophet is required by God to confront sin, even the sin of the king. It takes skill, wisdom, tact, courage and commitment to God to speak these words to the king. David, in his anger, could retaliate against Nathan and execute him. The prophet had to speak to David in a way that he would know this is his sin. Therefore, Nathan used a parable. A parable is an earthly story with a heavenly meaning. Often Jesus used parables, and Nathan chose this as his delivery method to get the message across to David. He felt David would be more open to receive God's message in a story.

Nathan, the Prophet's Story

There were two men in a town. One man was rich, and one man was poor. The rich man owned many sheep and cattle. The poor man owned nothing, except one little lamb. He raised that little lamb. It grew up with his children. It ate from the man's plate. It drank from his cup. He cuddled it in his arms like a baby. One day a guest arrived at the home of the rich man. Instead of killing an animal from his own flock or herd, he took the poor man's lamb, killed it and prepared it as a feast for his guest.

THE INTERPRETATION OF THE PARABLE

David was the rich man, king over all Israel. Uriah, a subject, an officer in his army, was the poor man. The many flocks and herds were symbolic of David's wives and concubines, which were many. David even had his master's Saul's wives at his disposal, if he wanted them. Uriah had one wife, Bathsheba. Bathsheba was much younger than he; therefore, she's described as a little lamb. Uriah paid a dowry to his wife and to her father. He nourished Bathsheba, as he did his own body. She was bone of his bone and flesh of his flesh. The two became one. He believed, whom God had put together, let no man divide asunder. He treated her, like he treated himself. He fed and cared for her, as he did his own body. He ate and drank with her. He cuddled her in his arms, as an expression of his love. He showed her true affection, kindness, and tenderness, as her husband. She was a partaker of all that he had. She was his family.

Prophet Nathan confronts David's sin of theft, adultery and murder. Nathan helped David realize that David himself would not tolerate that type behavior from anyone else in Israel. The sin Nathan describes was theft. David stole something from Uriah, just as the rich man stole from the poor man.

The wife hath not power of her own body, but the husband: and likewise also the husband hath not power of his own body, but the wife.   (I Corinthians 7:4) KJV

In a marriage, husband and wife compromise together concerning their bodies. David did not have authority over the body of Bathsheba. She was not his wife. He stole another man's wife body. David took something that did not belong to him. The nudity of another man's wife did not belong to David.

Satan, the tempter, is the traveler that came to David and stimulated his lust. Satan roamed to and fro and walked along with David, upon that roof, seeking to devour him. Satan is considered the wayfaring man. He follows a process after he finds the one he can devour. He proceeds in planting schemes, strategies and deceptions for sin. His aim is to rule David's spiritual house (body). Satan (wayfaring man) sits in the spiritual house, until he is needed for full manifestation of sin. He successfully confused the rich man, which is David. The rich man thinks he is operating under his normal behavior. Therefore, he stole a wife or lamb for the pleasure of Satan. David's heart was filled with lust at the sight of Bathsheba. In his selfishness, he did not get one of his own flock, wives, or concubines to satisfy himself. Instead, David took the poor man's only lamb or wife and prepared it for himself. In reality, he prepared the lamb or Bathsheba for Satan. In other words, he sent for Bathsheba and lay with her to gratify his lust.

5And David's anger was greatly kindled against the man; and he said to Nathan, As the Lord liveth, the man that hath done this thing shall surely die: 6And he shall restore the lamb fourfold, because he did this thing, and because he had no pity.
(2 Samuel 12:5-6) KJV

As Nathan told the story, David was furious and considered this a serious crime. He felt the rich man should not have taken the poor man's lamb. Any man that did such a thing deserved to die. According to the Law of Moses, a man had to compensate for the lamb fourfold, but not die for it. Nathan did not ask David for a lawful decision but received it from him anyway. He instantaneously pronounces a sentence of "guilty" on the rich man. David bamboozled by Satan, as well as his flesh, was not thinking spiritually. In his natural thinking, he assumed the story was true. He did not realize God sent the prophet for a Divine purpose.

David in a well of hypocrisy brought out his religious judgment. He tried to rid his guilty conscience by judging someone else. David's anger was affected by his own guilty conscience, that he ruled a death sentence for the rich man, though the crime was not a capital crime. David's use of the oath *"as the Lord lives"* shows how passionate he was about this wrong. He called God to witness the death sentence pronounced upon the rich man. David knew penalizing the rich man, even with death, wasn't right. According to the Law, the rich man had to restore fourfold to the poor man. David's words for a four-fold restoration indicate his sin and hardness of heart did not reduce his knowledge of the Word.

If a man steals an ox or a sheep, and slaughters it or sells it, he shall restore five oxen for an ox and four sheep for a sheep.
(Exodus 22:1) NKJV

David knew the Word but was still distant from God. When scripture says, "Because he had no pity", this meant the rich man should have had pity on his neighbor but did not. This applies the same way to David, a rich man, should have had pity on Uriah, but did not.

7 And Nathan said to David, Thou art the man. Thus saith the Lord God of Israel, I anointed thee king over Israel, and I delivered thee out of the hand of Saul; 8 And I gave thee thy master's house, and I gave thee thy master's wives into thy bosom, and I gave thee the house of Israel and of Judah; and if that had been too little, I would moreover have given unto thee such and such hings. 9Wherefore hast thou despised the commandment of the Lord, to do evil in his sight? thou hast killed Uriah the Hittite with the sword, and hast taken his wife to be thy wife, and hast slain him with the sword of the children of Ammon.

10Now therefore the sword shall never depart from thine house; because thou hast despised me, and hast taken the wife of Uriah the Hittite to be thy wife. 11Thus saith the Lord, Behold, I will raise up evil against thee out of thine own house, and I will take thy wives before thine eyes, and give them unto thy neighbour, and he shall lie with thy wives in the sight of this sun. 12For thou didst it secretly: but I will do this thing before all Israel, and before the sun.   (2 Samuel 12:7-12) KJV

GOD DECIDED TO PIERCE DAVID'S WORLD OF DARKNESS

God said to David, "Thou art the man; the rich man. Thou art the man!" That meant that this situation is similar to the woman at the well situation, in John 4. She had many husbands as David had many wives, but the one spouse they both were with; were not theirs. Thou art the man that stole this man only lamb or wife. Thou art the man." These were the powerful words that Nathan chose, to drive this parable home to David. He continued, saying to David, "This is the evil you have done, David. You have killed Uriah. You have taken his wife. You have committed this wrong." God refuse to let

David blame anyone or anything else. These words laid the foundation for what Nathan had to say next; "Thus said the LORD God of Israel".

THE PROSECUTION OF DAVID

He began with the words, "Thou are the man". Nathan, the Prophet of wisdom, sounded the alarm, so David could hear clearly. He shocked David into seeing his own sin. David became so insensitive to his own sins; he did not realize he was the villain in Nathan's story. David conscience had been seared as with a hot iron. The sharp disapproval of David's behavior begins the prophet's discourse with,

"THOU ART THE MAN"

God spiritually arrested David with this sentencing. Just as we see a man naturally arrested, so it was in the spirit. God placed David in a holding pattern, restricting movement and speech, so he could hear God's Word. God spiritually handcuffed his hands, placed spiritual shackles on his feet, and spiritual wired his mouth shut. These spiritual acts prevented David from moving or speaking while the prophet spoke. He sat in silence, as Nathan delivered a brief message; the words had Divine Power.

Is not my word like as a fire? saith the LORD; and like a hammer that breaketh the rock in pieces?
(Jeremiah 23:29) KJV

Hebrews 4:12 KJV says, *For the word of God is quick, and powerful, and sharper than any two-edged sword, piercing even to the dividing asunder of soul and spirit, and of the joints and marrow, and is a discerner of the thoughts and intents of the heart.*

The power of God's Word is a reprimand for the verdict of sin. Nathan offered this parable as sin existing in another person. When people talk about what another has done, the ear of the listener is wide open. People usually listen with interest when they are hearing something others have done. They give their undivided attention. Nothing breaks their concentration. Therefore, Nathan knew the flesh of the hearer would not get in the way, if impersonated in this manner. David could not deny that it was he.

God proceeded to remind David of His faithfulness. He supplied all of David's needs, according to His riches in glory. Thus saith, the Lord God of Israel; "I anointed thee king over Israel." He anointed David on three different occasions for this position of King. God said, "I delivered thee out of the hand of Saul." There were many times Saul tried to kill David. God protected and spared his life. God said, "I gave thee thy master's house." God gave Saul's entire household and property with all it entails to David. God continued reminding David, "I gave thee thy master's wives into thy bosom." According to the law, the king had a right to his predecessor's wives. God gave him every female servant and courtesans. Many women attended to the needs of this rich and powerful man. This royal harem was a part of the royal inheritance. Another reminder to David from God, "I gave thee the house of Israel and of Judah." God gave these kingdoms to David, so he could be king over the twelve tribes of Israel.

When God used the word "such and such", He was explaining to David, that if there were anything that had no name, or anything that has never been specified, God would give it to him. If David wanted anything that had no name, God would have created it just for David. God was saying, "If there were not enough women or wives for you, I would have given you more. If the kingdom was not big enough, I would expand it. If my favors were not enough I would have given you greater favors! I had so much more to give you in your future, but you chose to sin instead."

God reminded David, "If all the above things had been too little, I would have given unto thee "such and such things". When God used the word "such and such", He was explaining to David, that if there were anything that had no name or anything that has never been specified, God would give it to him. If David wanted anything that had no name, God would have created it just for David. God is saying, "If there were not enough women or wives for you, I would have given you more. If the kingdom was not big enough, I would expand it. If my favors were not enough I would have given you greater favors. I had so much more to give you in your future, but you chose to sin instead."

From whence come wars and fightings among you? Come they not hence, even of your lusts that war in your members? Ye lust, and have not: ye kill, and desire to have, and cannot obtain: ye fight and war; yet ye have not, because ye ask not. (James 4:1-2) KJV

    Notice in the scripture God identified Bathsheba as the wife of Uriah the Hittite. God did not use Bathsheba's name. He wanted David to realize Bathsheba as the wife of Uriah. The words, the wife of Uriah, the Hittite, were designed to resound or echo in the ears and mind of David for a long time. God mentioned in verses nine and ten that David took Uriah's, the Hittite's wife, and made her his wife. God was very displeased about this event.

    Through Nathan, God explained to David that his sin indicated he was ungrateful for all God had done to and for him. When God's word is despised, it is despising God. In 2 Samuel 12, God specifically said David despised the commandment of the LORD. In other words, David took God and His words for granted. God and His Word are ONE! His Word says. "Thou shalt not kill". But David killed Uriah. The commandment says, "Thou shall not covet your neighbor's wife". David coveted Uriah's his neighbor's wife. The commandment says, "Thou shall not commit adultery." David committed adultery. The commandment says, "Thou shall not steal." David stole another man's wife. The Word of God remind us that David took the sword of an Ammonite to kill Uriah. Although David's own sword was clean, there was still blood on his hands. David took this dead man's wife and made her his wife.

David's punishment was a promise and a prophecy from God. It was guarantee to happen. David's sin was private, but God made his discipline and correction public. From that day forward David would inherit recognized violence and bloodshed among his own family. Bloodshed will persist, all the days of David's life. God's Word says, "I will raise up rebellion against you from your own house. Because you troubled another man's house, I will allow trouble to come from within your own house. I will take your wives before your eyes. As you violated another man's wife, another will violate your wives. Your own family will bring adversity against you." Here is a small summary of the promise and prophesies from God to David.

IT CAME TO PASS

Her brother Amnon raped Tamar, David's daughter. Absalom had sexual relations with his father's concubines, on the same roof David had lusted after Bathsheba. Israel watched as Absalom did this. The deaths of Amnon and Absalom were violent. Absalom set up Amnon to get drunk and had him murdered. Later, ten young men surrounded Absalom, murdered him, and casted his body into a hole in the woods. David's first child by Bathsheba died. David reaped what he had sowed. The words from God came to pass because David had sinned against God. David murdered Uriah and stole his wife.

Sin is pleasurable for a season. I imagine if David knew how much pain, the pleasure of sin would cause him; he would have reconsidered the thought. He may not have chased temporary pleasures.

13And David said unto Nathan, I have sinned against the Lord. And Nathan said unto David, The Lord also hath put away thy sin; thou shalt not die.14Howbeit, because by this deed thou hast given great occasion to the enemies of the Lord to blaspheme, the child also that is born unto thee shall surely die.
(2 Samuel 12:13-14) KJV

David's acknowledgment and confession is a good example. He placed the blame on his own shoulders. David realized he had sinned against God. Could it be that the few words, "I have sinned against the LORD" reveals how broken David really was? He offered no excuses for his sin. He is not hiding his sin. He is not looking for a way out for his sin. He is not saying that God knows his heart. He is not saying his flesh was weak. David didn't use enticing words of man's wisdom to get out of this. He did not deny the truth but acknowledged his guilt openly and honestly. This is the exposed humility of a man in David's high position.

God is working on David's heart. Nathan's part was just the last step of God's work. In all this, David is revealed as a man after God's own heart. Other kings may have tried to cover up or preserved their behavior. Instead of admitting their sin, they would have killed the prophet. David would not stoop to that level. He loved God too much and knew he had wronged God. David confessed that he sinned. Change happened, when he realized he needed change. He had to deal with his sin against the LORD. That's how vast his sin is. His sin against Bathsheba, against Uriah, against his wives, children and against the nation were big. But, his sin against the LORD was greatest of all. David's confession created the writing of Psalm 51, "I have sinned against the LORD."

AFTER DAVID REPENTED, NATHAN ANNOUNCED GOD'S INSTANT FORGIVENESS

There were no addendums attached. He was not on probation. God's process of restoration is opposite from man's law. Man's laws place a person on probation, after they are released from jail. When God told David that he would not die, He exonerated David. The penalty for adultery under the Law of Moses was death. David believed the Word of the prophet, "Thou art the man!" Therefore, he believed the Word of the prophet when he said, "The Lord also has put away your sin; you shall not die"! David deserved the death penalty for adultery and murder. But God's grace bypassed His own plan for punishment.

David cursed the LORD by doing what the world

does. This sin could make them ignore God's Word. David was God's visible representative and ambassador in the earth. He was supposed to be a living epistle read and seen of men. People should want to come to God because of his lifestyle. Yet, the opposite happened. David fell, and the world watched. Therefore, in the mind of the world, why should they follow God? He caused others to stumble. All of David's scheming could not hide his sin from the world. Whatever is done in the dark will come to light. The world knew.

Howbeit, because by this deed thou hast given great occasion to the enemies of the Lord to blaspheme, the child also that is born unto thee shall surely die.   (2 Samuel 12:14) KJV

You shall not die, but the child born from this adulterous and murderous strategy will die. The child will die due to David cursing of God before the world. This is not a judgment on the child for being conceived out of wedlock. It is a judgment on David for his sin. The child's death was tragic, but causing a nation to stumble, and die due to the king's sin life is tragic also. God pardoned David and Bathsheba lives. He took their child instead of taking them. Although David's sin was forgiven, the child was born from his adultery. The LORD could not ignore David's sins. If God did that, it would give unbelievers an opportunity to say God of Israel is not Holy. The world saw the leader as a hypocrite and saying one thing and doing another thing.

They would say Israel's God accepts the sinful life of His king.

God forgave the king but did not defend him from the outcome of the sin. David had to face consequences for his sin. Consequences began with the death of the child. It is never seen in scripture that David repeated this sin again. Psalm 32 describes perfectly the spiritual struggle David encountered when God began to deal heavily with him. David had physically sinned, but his deep agony was because he sinned against God.

1Blessed is he whose transgression is forgiven, whose sin is covered. 2Blessed is the man unto whom the Lord imputeth not iniquity, and in whose spirit there is no guile. 3When I kept silence, my bones waxed old through my roaring all the day long. 4For day and night thy hand was heavy upon me: my moisture is turned into the drought of summer. Selah. 5I acknowledge my sin unto thee, and mine iniquity have I not hid. I said, I will confess my transgressions unto the Lord; and thou forgavest the iniquity of my sin. Selah.

6For this shall every one that is godly pray unto thee in a time when thou mayest be found: surely in the floods of great waters they shall not come nigh unto him. 7Thou art my hiding place; thou shalt preserve me from trouble; thou shalt compass me about with songs of deliverance. Selah. 8I will instruct thee and teach thee in the way which thou shalt go: I will guide thee with mine eye. 9Be ye not as the horse, or as the mule, which have no understanding: whose mouth must be held in with bit and bridle, lest they come near unto thee. 10Many sorrows shall be to the wicked: but he that trusteth in the Lord, mercy shall compass him about. 11Be glad in the Lord, and rejoice, ye righteous: and shout for joy, all ye that are upright in heart.   (Psalms 32:1-11) AKJV

15And Nathan departed unto his house. And the Lord struck the child that Uriah's wife bare unto David, and it was very sick. 16David therefore besought God for the child; and David fasted, and went in, and lay all night upon the earth. 17And the elders of his house arose, and went to him, to raise him up from the earth: but he would not, neither did he eat bread with them.

18And it came to pass on the seventh day, that the child died. And the servants of David feared to tell him that the child was dead: for they said, Behold, while the child was yet alive, we spake unto him, and he would not hearken unto our voice: how will he then vex himself, if we tell him that the child is dead? 19But when David saw that his servants whispered, David perceived that the child was dead: therefore David said unto his servants, Is the child dead? And they said, He is dead. 20Then David arose from the earth, & washed, and anointed himself, and changed his apparel, and came into the house of the Lord, and worshipped: then he came to his own house; and when he required, they set bread before him, &he did eat.

21Then said his servants unto him, What thing is this that thou hast done? thou didst fast & weep for the child, while it was alive; but when the child was dead, thou didst rise and eat read. 22And he said, While the child was yet alive, I fasted and wept: for I said,

Who can tell whether God will be gracious to me, that the child may live? 23But now he is dead, wherefore should I fast? can I bring him back again? I shall go to him, but he shall not return to me.   (2 Samuel 12:15-23) KJV

Even though Uriah was dead, and David was legally married to Bathsheba, the Word of God still refers to Bathsheba as Uriah's wife. The reason is, when the child was conceived, Uriah was alive, and Bathsheba was Uriah's wife. It is God's way of saying, "Uriah's death and the marriage following his death, does not brand everything as okay. Since the child's sickness came immediately after the words of Nathan, the prophet, it was received as the Ordained Hand of God. The severe sickness came upon the child immediately. It was interpreted by the king as the execution of the first stage of death's process. The child suffered for several days and the correction was heavy upon David and Bathsheba; not the child.

David pleaded with God for grace and mercy for the child. He resorted to fasting after he was told the child would die. David continued many days and night fasting, praying, weeping and mourning. He sought God desperately for the child. He even slept on the floor prostrate before God. The heart of David was in agony over the suffering of his son. I imagine in prayer and fasting, David could reflect on his life of sin. He prayed for a clean heart and a renewed spirit. He surrendered his life and the child's life totally to God. He said, "Not my will, but thou will be done O God"! He may have felt God may be gracious toward him. God just may be gracious toward the child. I can see David probably reminiscencing over the Word of God. He took a journey while in prayer looking over the many times God was gracious to His patriots. He thought, maybe God may be gracious to the child, as He had been to David in the previous verses. After all, with God all things are possible.

David's prayer and fasting did not force God to change His mind, His plan or His hand. Prayer and fasting did place David in a position to receive what he should from God. Prayer and fasting was designed to place David in position to apprehend spiritual blessings. David's spiritual blessings would be the peace of God that will surpass all understanding. This peace will keep his heart and his mind. The baby did not live long enough to be named. He died on the seventh day. Seven is the number of God's completion. The number seven indicated it is over.

The elders were David's senior officials and in his royal court. They were afraid to say anything to their master. They had observed the magnitude and intensity of his grief before the baby died. They anticipated their master would be in an uncontrollable rage once he learned of the child's death. The elders were astonished by David's behavior. David had a sense of peace when the child died. He had done all he could to seek God's mercy in this time of punishment.

The teacher in David emerges for those that needed to be taught. He taught them a lesson of leading by example, as well as, what he said. He told the elders, his mourning the dead, would only increase his anguish of bereavement with added misery. Therefore, David arose from the earth. He arose out of his flesh and washed himself. He washed himself with the washing of the water of the Word. He anointed himself. He anointed himself with the oil of gladness. He changed his clothes. He changed his clothes to his robe of righteousness. He went into the House of the LORD and worshipped God. He did not forsake assembling himself in the house of God. He enters God's courts with praise. He was thankful unto Him and blessed His name. For the Lord is good. His mercy endureth forever. He went into worship of the Almighty God, who turned his mourning into dancing. His worship now takes on a different character from the worship he offered God in weeping and mourning.

His worship expressed total commitment and submission of his will to God's will. He acknowledged God's loving kindness and righteous judgment. David's ability to worship and honor God in a time of trial and crisis demonstrates spiritual confidence. David explained to his elders the uselessness of further fasting and weeping. The child was dead. There is nothing he could do about it. He said, the dead cannot return to life. The living can go to the dead, but the dead cannot come back to the living. Could David now have a knowing in his spiritual heavenly mind that he shall see his son again when he went to heaven.

24And David comforted Bathsheba his wife, and went in unto her, and lay with her: and she bare a SON, and he called his name Solomon: and the Lord loved him.25 And he sent by the hand of Nathan the prophet; and He called his name Jedidiah, because of the Lord.   (Samuel 12:24-25) KJV

    Notice, after David was corrected for his sin, God calls Bathsheba for the first time, David's wife. We can say Bathsheba was going through a hard time as well, though it was never mentioned. She had to mourn and buried two deaths in one year. I am sure she had to face her part in the events, as well. Scripture says David comforted her. Maybe he comforted her by saying God has forgiven us of our sin.

    God gave them another son. This son was heir to David's throne. He was Jesus' ancestor that demonstrated God forgives us of sin. This son shall build the house of God. He called his name Solomon; which means peace. Therefore, David had peace, once the baby died. Solomon name means "Peace." God had filled David's inward parts with a seed called "Peace". This "Peace" was the spiritual blessing set-aside for him in heavenly places, Solomon! Once David went into his wife to lay with her; peace was release from his inward parts. God was faithful to David to continue that Peace. The LORD loved David and Solomon. God was not going to take this child, as he had the first child. The birth of this son was God's confirmation of the reconciliation between God, David and Bathsheba.

26 And Joab fought against Rabbah of the children of Ammon, and took the royal city. 27 And Joab sent messengers to David, and said, I have fought against Rabbah, and have taken the city of waters. 28 Now therefore gather the rest of the people together, and encamp against the city, and take it: lest I take the city, and it be called after my name.

29 And David gathered all the people together, and went to Rabbah, and fought against it, and took it. 30 And he took their king's crown from off his head, the weight whereof was a talent of gold with the precious stones: and it was set on David's head. And he brought forth the spoil of the city in great abundance. 31 And he brought forth the people that were therein, and put them under saws, and under harrows of iron, and under axes of iron, and made them pass through the brick-kiln: and thus did he unto all the cities of the children of Ammon. So David and all the people returned unto Jerusalem.   (2 Samuel 12:26-31) KJV

    Joab fought against Rabbah, and was about to complete the defeat, so he encouraged King David to return to battle. He said, "I want you to take all the credit for defeating Rabba and capturing the Ammon people. "Come and finish this war". Joab struggled for over one year to conquer Rabbah. Victory came when David got right with God. It was the spiritual reason behind the lack of victory at Rabbah. David's sin at home hindered

Joab's success. David had been out of position as a king, not at war. Sin hindered the defeat of Rabbah; now ready to be taken. It was David's arrival with his elite troops that won the victory. David captured the city, took the spoil, and set the people to forced labor.

This was the final phase of David's restoration when he went back and did what he was supposed to do

He led Israel out to battle, instead of remaining in Jerusalem. David refocused, moved back into position and won battles. Sin did not condemn him to a life of failure and defeat. It was his punishment for sin; but it was not designed to destroy his life. The gold placed upon David's head is symbolic of being tried by the refiner's fire, removing all the dross and coming out as pure gold. His righteousness was as pure gold again. He was focused; God was pleased!

Eventually, the crown was placed upon David's head. This was symbolic of David taking his God ordained authority as king. It was symbolic to him getting back into position. Also, the abundance of spoil, David took was sowed and dedicated to the building of the house of God by His Son named Peace; Solomon!

30And he took their king's crown from off his head, the weight whereof was a talent of gold with the precious stones: and it was set on David's head. And he brought forth the spoil of the city in great abundance. (2 Samuel 12:30) KJV

8th APPROACH

The Woman at the Well Made to Focus for the Other Side Ministry

Another one of Jesus' important assignment required Him to go to the *other side* to Samaria. His mission was to pierce the darkness of a woman with an identity crisis. He had to free her from a spirit of whoredom, so her focus could be restored. Jesus had to penetrate her world that she may become Full of Consistent and Unlimited Sight for the things of God.

She had been called from her mother's womb. God put forth His hand and touched her mouth. He said unto her, "Behold, I have put my words in thy mouth. See I have set thee over the nations and over the kingdoms, to root out, and to pull down, and to destroy, and to throw down, to build and to plant. You are called to become the *other side* minister that is focused."

But ye shall receive power, after that the Holy Ghost is come upon you: and ye shall be witnesses unto me both in Jerusalem, and in all Judaea, and in Samaria, and unto the uttermost part of the earth.   (Acts 1:8) KJV

THIS IS THE *OTHER SIDE* MINISTRY

Behold, I give unto you power to tread on serpents and scorpions, and over all the power of the enemy: and nothing shall by any means hurt will you.   *(Luke 10:19) KJV*

The *other side* ministry is the world's territory; unsaved, gangs, prostitutes, identity crisis, liars, cheaters, adulterer, homeless, sick and those that have been good all their lives but have not received Jesus.

When therefore the Lord knew how the Pharisees had heard that Jesus made and baptized more disciples than John; though Jesus Himself had baptized none but his disciples, He left Judea and departed again into Galilee.   *(John 4:1-3) KJV*

According to scriptures, John the Baptist popularity began to decrease. The religious systems of the Pharisees resented Jesus, because His popularity started to increase. This opposition rose even more against Jesus because He moved out to establish the other side ministry. The Gospel of the Kingdom that He preached challenged their teachings.

Jesus had just begun His ministry of sharing the Good News. According to the timing of God, it was not the time or season to confront the Pharisees openly. Jesus did not want a crisis, so He left Judea and went to Galilee. He left the religious leaders to deal with the futility, uselessness and ineffectiveness of their own mind. Jesus raised a standard.

And He must needs go through Samaria. (John 4:4) KJV

Jesus had a divine appointment in Samaria; it was for the *other side* ministry. He was so greatly consumed by the

business of His Father, that the desire and passion inside of Him was called, "a must need". His mission was on the *other side*. The issues the religious leaders used to stir Him earlier were abortion tactics. Sometimes oppositions in life will arise and are designed to abort the ministry on the *other side*.

THE *OTHER SIDE* IS CONSIDERED THE SIDE WHERE BELIEVERS ARE NOT PARTS OF THAT WORLD

The *other side* is the place of assignment where, Satan does not want believers and souls to have victory. Jesus' *other side* ministry involved a woman with a root system called the works of the flesh. The works of her flesh was evident. Works of the flesh are designed to make everything else in a person's life more important than a meaningful relationship with Jesus. The book of Galatians said it well in chapter 5.

Now the works of the flesh are evident: sexual immorality, impurity, sensuality, idolatry, sorcery, enmity, strife, jealousy, fits of anger, rivalries, dissensions, divisions, envy, drunkenness, orgies, and things like these. (Galatians 5:19-21) KJV

This woman was known according to her fleshly life. Matthew chapter 7 speaks about knowing people by their fruit.

Therefore, by their fruit you shall know them.
(Matthew 7:20) KJV

The "must need" is the calling and conversion of a woman that is controlled by the strongman, whoredom.

Some manifested spirits of whoredom are unfaithfulness, adultery, fornication, chronic dissatisfaction, excessive appetite and worldliness. We also see there is a "must need" to convert other Samaritans, that are on the *other side*.

The Father gave Jesus these people. Therefore, He was determined to go this way. The *other side* ministry must be built in Samaria. He had to reveal Himself as a Jew that was greater than the prophet Jacob and as the Messiah. Jesus chose this direct route to immediately get to this woman. Usually, Jews took the longest route, which was five days, to get to that area. They went through the hot desert to Jericho, from Jerusalem, up north to the Jordan River valley and east toward Galilee. This route that Jesus took was seventy miles, and two and a half days walking. Jesus again disregards the normalcy of doing things the way others did things.

Jews were prejudice against the Samaritans. After the Assyrians conquered the Northern Kingdom, they imported people into Samaritans. Some Jews married the importees. The pure Jews hated this mixed race called Samarians. They felt interracial marriages polluted their people, nation and faith. Jesus, a Jew had no reason to live by their cultural restrictions. The route through Samaria was shorter and He took it. Jesus proves the *other side* ministry had no place for racial prejudices and barriers. The *other side* ministry is a spiritual thing, and racial prejudice is a natural thing. The *other side* ministry focused on destroying the culture of racial barriers and prejudice.

> *Then cometh he to a city called Samaria, which is called Sychar near to the parcel of ground that Jacob gave unto his son Joseph. Now Jacob's well was there. Jesus therefore being wearied with his journey sat thus on the well: and it was about the sixth hour.*
> *(John 4:5-6) KJV*

Jesus became tired, hot and thirsty around the sixth hour. In Jew's time, it was noon; in Roman time, this was evening. He sat on a cold, hard well to be refreshed from walking to the *other side* ministry. The *other side* ministry does not always offer the best transportation. This is one of the ways Jesus is teaching His disciples. He uses his feet as His reliable transportation. The key is being content in whatever state we are in. It is a part of the *other side* ministry.

> *There cometh a woman of Samaria to draw water: Jesus said unto her, give me to drink. For his disciples were gone away unto the city to buy meat.* *(John 4:9-10) KJV*

Now we see Jesus entering the purpose for the *other side* ministry. This is where Jesus shows us one of the foolish things that God will use to confound the wise. This is a picture of God's favor upon this woman in seed form. She does not seem qualified for what He called her to do. God bypassed many religious leaders, to get to this woman, controlled by a spirit of whoredom. Does this seem foolish or what? Jesus understood, there are many *other side* ministers in the womb of this *other side* woman.

First, let's go over her qualifications for the *other side* ministry

She is infamous and offensive to the town. She qualifies. She is the most gossiped about woman in this area. She qualifies. She is the only woman at the well to draw water. She qualifies. Women usually drew water at the same time, but not with her. Where were the other women? She qualifies. Her reputation causes her to visit the well when others did not. She did this to prevent stares and looks. She qualifies. The elite women of society refused to fellowship with her kind. She qualifies. She was not popular with these women, but she was popular with their husbands and other men. She qualifies.

Through Divine guidance, it was no accident she went to the well. It was purposed. During those times, meeting at the well had much significance. Rebekah met Isaac at the well, Rachel met Jacob at the well and Jethro's daughter met Moses at the well. Now this woman met Jesus, her real husband, at the well. She went to the well, but she did not expect to get the living water.

Jesus sent the disciples for meat. He was a master spiritual strategist. He did not want his disciples to abort what God wanted to do in this future *other side* minister. When purpose is not understood, it can be aborted. For instance, Judas and Peter walked with Jesus. They had no idea an abortionist spirit could try to influence them. Satan tried to use them for his purpose to perform an abortion. Many abortionists, unknowingly, are under a spirit of deception. The purpose of a spirit of deception is to seduce and abort God's plan in the earth. For this cause, Jesus ministered to this woman alone. He refused to further damage her through embarrassment or shame. He had no desire to reveal her sin life to them. Therefore, He spoke to her in private. Jesus had to lay the foundation of the *other side* ministry.

Jesus, the Water of Life, asks the woman to give Him a drink. Let us examine His strategy for the other side ministry. First, He strikes up a conversation. Jesus had a stronger, more violent thirst for this woman's soul, salvation and welfare. Let us look at an example. Whenever a person gives an invitation for another person to go out, and have a drink with them, it is to start a conversation. The purpose is to develop a meaningful relationship. Jesus did not think it was robbery to minister to one person, instead of multitudes. Neither, did He think it robbery to minister to a woman, not of His social status. She was a stranger as well as a Samaria woman. In the *other side* ministry, the one is just as important to Jesus as the many. Jesus understood that all God's people must be ministered to, no matter what occupation or personality they have.

Then said the woman of Samaria unto Him, how is it that thou being a Jew asketh drink of me, which am a woman of Samaria? For the Jews have no dealings with the Samarians. Jesus answered

and said unto her, if thou knewest the gift of God and who it is that saith unto thee Give Me to drink; thou wouldest have asked of Him and He would have given thee living water.
(John 4:9-10) AKJV

The Jews hated the Samarians more than they hated the Gentiles. They hated their religious practices and mixing the Law of Moses with idolatry. They felt the Samaritans defiled Jewish faith. Therefore, the woman was surprised Jesus, a Jew, spoke with her, by asking for water. She answers Him with a question. "How is it that thou being a Jew asketh drink of me, which am a woman of Samaria?" Basically, she was saying to Jesus, "I am supposed to be disgusting to You. Jews refuse any kindness or fellowship from Samaritans". They rather face any type of hardship than to be caught with a Samaritan. Instead, Jesus ignored her words concerning the Jews. He decides to use this water at hand to teach her a lesson. Jesus moved toward his purpose of being there; the *other side* ministry. He was saying to her, "If you knew who I AM". If you could see me as more than a Jew. If you could see ME as more than a tired traveler". If you knew your day of visitation, when your eyes are opened, you will see, I Am the Gift of God! He was saying, I am the Son of God manifested in the flesh and dwell among men. I emptied Myself and became human, to ask you for water. Asking water from you is a gift within itself. Just sow a seed of a little water to reap a supernatural supply of Living Water forever. It is more blessed to give than receive. I am the Gift of God, the only begotten son of My Father. I am your Gift, source for your life, and Living Water. Rivers of Living Water will flow from you as it does from ME. My Living Water will satisfy your thirst for the world".

LIVING WATER IS AN ORDAINED STRATEGY OF THE *OTHER SIDE* MINISTRY

It is a gift and whoever receives it, will flow. A gift is a present used, admired, love, adored, shown and remembered; we should just take the gift.

The woman said unto Him Sir, thou hast nothing to draw with and the well is deep; from whence hast thou this living water? Art thou greater than our Father Jacob, which gave us the well and drank thereof himself and his children and cattle?
(John 4:11-12) KJV

The woman misunderstood Jesus. She was limited by her thoughts. He was thinking naturally but speaking spiritually. Spiritual things are foolishness to the natural man. She respects Him by saying, "Sir". Yet, she does not respect what He was saying. There was something similar on the inside of her, which was on the inside of the man with 6000 demons. That same breath of life that kept the man at the Ganderenes alive until Jesus arrived, also kept her going until Jesus arrived. The breath made her relate to Jesus. After all, she was created in the image of God. He blew the breath of life into her. His life was on the inside her. She really did not understand how He could give her this water. She was thinking of water from a reservoir; well. When the reservoir is reached, water flows. She says, "There is nothing to draw with, or no bucket to put water in". But this fountain of life must be received and not drawn; the fountain is Christ.

JESUS OTHER SIDE MINISTER TAPS INTO HER THIRST MECHANISM

In the natural, regular water intake varies from one person to another. It is strongly influenced by habit. Water intake comes in the form of liquids, foods and cell metabolism, as food and liquids, which are broken down. Water output occurs through lungs exhalation, skin, perspiration, feces and urine. Healthy people know how to maintain body fluids. Thirst is a driving force for water intake. When water volume decreases in the body, it results in dry mouth. It triggers the thirst center motivating us to drink fluids. Thirst is quenched as soon as water is consumed. Dehydration occurs when more water is lost, than is taken in. Severe dehydration can cause death.

In the spiritual, Living Water intake varies from one person to another. It is strongly influenced by habit. Living Water intake occurs in the form of Salvation, Word of God, church attendance, faith, bible study, prayer, praise, worship, gifts, fellowship etc. Living Water output occurs when a person become part of the other side ministry. We minister salvation, love, teach, preach, witness, testify, become epistles, manifestation of gifts, praying for others, praising, worshipping and living a Christian lifestyle. Healthy *other side* ministers and people, know how to maintain their Living Water intake. Thirst for God is their driving force for Living Water intake. When the volume of Living Water decreases, it results in dry mouth.

Dry mouth is symbolic to fulfilling the lust of the flesh, leaving the things of God, no prayer life, not reading bible, no church or bible study, no fellowship with saints, etc. Thirst is quenched when we start drinking the Living Water. Dehydration occurs when more Living Water is lost than we are taking in. Severe spiritual dehydration can cause spiritual death.

13Jesus answered and said unto her, Whosoever, shall drink of this water shall thirst again; 14But whosoever shall drinketh of the water that I shall give him shall never thirst; but the water that I shall give him shall be in him a well of water springing up into everlasting life. 15The woman saith unto him, Sir give me this water that I thirst not, neither cometh hither to draw.
(John 4:13-15) AKJV

THE OTHER SIDE MINISTRY EXPLANATION FOR THIRST

THIRST AGAIN - Jesus is saying; Jacob's water is transient, and it is temporary. It will not last long. Drinking this well water, or any water will cause desire for more water. You will thirst again. Whatever you use to quench any thirst in life, it will cause you to thirst again. Water quenches thirst and refreshes for a little while. Earthly desires that quench thirst is transient. It will NOT last long. In time, you must drink again, due to rise in body temperature. This is symbolic of dissatisfaction. Earthly desires bring temporary satisfaction. This woman knew about thirsting again because she came to the well daily.

NEVER THIRST AGAIN – Jesus answered in a wise and gentle manner while instructing her. The water Jesus has will not cause her to thirst again. Jesus water have will fill, moisturize and preserve her. It will give her a quality of life she has never experienced before. It will flow from her belly as Living Water. It will activate the *other side* ministry within her. It is Acts 1:8 manifested in the flesh to dwell among her expressed. It will be unlimited waters flowing like a fountain from the eternal life of God. It will be unlimited waters as it swells into a river from the eternal life of God. It will be unlimited waters as it expands into an ocean from the eternal life of God. It has Divine satisfaction.

Just as the local water system has a faucet to turn on and deliver water; she will have a Divine water system that is turned on to deliver Living Water. Both have a reserved supply. Jesus has a 24-hour delivery system that is continuous, and never runs out. His system will remain and never die. The pipes will never burst. The meter does not need reading, as with natural meters. The homeowner will never receive a water bill cut off notice.

JESUS REALIZES THE WOMAN IN A STATE OF CONFUSION, THEREFORE, HE DECIDES TO PIERCE HER DARKNESS

The woman was confused, double minded and unstable. She asks where she should go to receive the Living Water. She probably was glad because this would stop her daily trips to the well. Jesus earlier explanation about Living Water did not faze her. She had no idea that she was operating under the authority of the kingdom of darkness.

The god of this age has blinded the minds of unbelievers, so that they cannot see the light of the gospel that displays the glory of Christ, who is the image of God. (2 Corinthians 4:4) KJV

She did not understand. Therefore, Jesus decided at that moment to rock her world, and pierced her darkness. The Word about the Living Water had to awaken her conscience and penetrate her life. Jesus had to open the wound of guilt to prick her heart. Jesus had to take it to the house she lived in. He had to do something to shatter her current secure world.

Jesus said, go call thy husband and come thither! The woman answered and said, "I have no husband." Jesus said unto her, thou hast well said, I have no husband; for thou hast had five husbands; and he whom thou now hast is not thy husband; in that saidst thou truly.   (John 4:16-18) KJV

Jesus is saying, "It is time for Him to go deeper." His deep must call unto her deep. This is the point Jesus moved in a Word of Knowledge about her present and past situation. Was she a widow? Had she abandon her husband? Was she a divorcee? Was she a fornicator? Whatever she was, it was no doubt, it was five husbands and Jesus said number six is a counterfeit. This woman had placed pressure upon many men to make her happy. But these six men seemed to have failed her. Oblivious to her, Jesus will become her number seventh man or husband. The number seven means completion; therefore, she will become completed once and for all. He will never leave nor forsake her. She will find Jesus with her in the morning when she awakens. It will not be as other men in the past; they all left her on the morning after.

Jesus commended her for telling the truth. She was truthful in saying she had no husband. Jesus knew everything about her. Why would a woman go from relationship to relationship or pursue five lovers and even live with a man that was not hers? What in the world was she looking for? Jesus had pierced her darkness and found her thirst mechanism. He knew she was thirsting for wholeness, relationships, protection, acceptance, affirmation, affection, healing, love and security.

Her thirst for men caused her to seek what she thought would make her alive. This was a smoke screen influenced by a spirit of whoredom. That spirit caused her to join herself to it and drank false living water. However, her thirst was never satisfied. Counterfeits dictated what she needed. Jesus saw her thirst for fleshy things had totally consumed her. Those things were compensations, which resulted in insanity. She did the same things but kept receiving the same results each time.

Jesus brought conviction as well as freedom into her life. This qualified her even more for the *other side* ministry. He penetrated her secret sins, denial and defenses. He penetrated the relationships that had controlled her, but still left her all alone.

17So now, no longer am I the one doing it, but sin which dwells in me. 18For I know that nothing good dwells in me, that is, in my flesh; for the willing is present in me, but the doing of the good is not. 19For the good that I want, I do not do, but I practice the very evil that I do not want. 20But if I am doing the very thing I do not want, I am no longer the one doing it, but sin which dwells in me. 21I find then the principle that evil is present in me, the one who wants to do good   (Romans 7:17-21) NASB

There were two struggles within her that war against each other; sin and life, flesh and spirit. One stopped her from doing right. She agreed with God's Word in her heart. But, there was something in every part of her body, fought against her mind. It made her a prisoner of sin and controlled everything she did. What a sad person she was. Who would rescue her from the body doomed to die? Christ Jesus rescues her for the *other side* ministry.

The woman said to Him sir I perceive that thou are a prophet. Our Fathers worshipped in this mountain and ye say that in

Jerusalem is the place where men ought to worship.

(John 4:19-20) KJV

This word "perceive" means to recognize, discern, understand, realize, sense, judge or consider YOU are a prophet. She said, "Sir I perceive, that is my spirit connects to your spirit. You are a prophet?" She was saying, "Sir, I perceive you are like Samuel. Samuel told Saul what was in his heart. You are like Elisha; Elisha told Gehazzi what was in his heart." She tried to change the subject to move attention from her. The prophet revealed her heart. He confronted her lukewarm life after He received revelation. He found her treasure, and therefore He found her heart. He saw whoredom sitting on the throne of her heart.

21 Jesus said unto her woman believe me, the hour is cometh when ye shall neither in this mountain nor yet at Jerusalem worship the Father. 22 Ye worship ye know not what; we know what we worship; for salvation is of the Jews. 23 But the houreth cometh and now is when the true worshipper shall worship the Father in Spirit and in truth; For the Father seeketh such to worship Him. 24 God is Spirit and they that worship Him must worship Him in spirit and in truth. *(John 4:21-24) KJV*

Jesus was saying, "Woman, this is the hour, true worship is going to come from you. True worship is going to engulf you sooner than you know. True worship from you is going to be within this hour. It will be in spirit, and it will be in truth. True worship must come so you can become effective for this *other side* ministry.

The gate for true worship is straight and narrow. It is harder to get through this narrow gate of true worship. Everyone cannot go. Worship agrees with God. God is spirit and has no natural body. He is free of limits of time and space. Our spirit must worship His spirit. God does not want traditional, formal, lifestyle, conduct or superstitious worship. Worship is a matter of the heart attitude toward God.

Locations, churches, or buildings are not the issue of true worship. Closing eyes, prayer, singing, serving, fast song, slow song, body exercise or lip service is not the issue for true worship. Body posture of kneeling knees, raised hands, hands in a prayer position, clapping hands, and bowing the head is not true worship. The body is God's temple, and that is where we worship Him. True worship is service to God when it is with deep affection and love for Him. God seeks, consumes, desire to find, probes, examines, and is searching for true worshippers. They are rare.

The woman left her water pot and went her way into the city and saith to the men, come see A MAN which told me all the things that ever I did: is not this the Christ.   John 4:28-29) KJV

The woman left her water pot, and quickly became one of the *other side* ministers! We can see the *other side* ministry in action within her. She became a church builder, an apostle and a witness of the Good News, an evangelist. She left the water pot because her old thirst was gone. She left what was symbolic of her old life. She left her old grave clothes. She was a new creation and old things had passed away. God makes all things new. She now has a new position in Christ as a new *other side* minister. She put on new clothes for her new position in Christ; a minister of the *other side* ministry. She received Living Water, and now wants to share it.

The woman in the *other side* ministry went immediately to potential *other side* ministers. She went to those she could relate to first; MEN! She was saying, "Hey men come and see a real man". He is not counterfeit or artificial, but He is genuine." They listened to her, not because of her sex, but because there was power in the words she spoke. The power of Living Water, and power of the Holy Ghost energized her words. The anointing arrested the men and made them be still. She was saying to these men, "You never told me all I ever did, as Jesus told me. Maybe it is because you are the ones who did it with me. Is He not the Christ?"

Jesus did not tell this woman everything she ever did. The power of his gaze penetrated her heart. She felt like Jesus knew the extent of everything she did. The prophet told her things only He and she knew. She was so deeply convicted that, she felt as though, He had revealed all she had ever done.

31In the mean while His disciples prayed Him, saying, Master, eat. 32But he said unto them, I have meat to eat that ye know not of (other side ministers to recruit). 33therefore said the disciples one to another, Hath any man brought him ought to eat? 34 Jesus saith unto them, My meat is to do the will of him that sent me, and to finish his work. (John 4:31-34) KJV

In verse 8, the disciples went to town for meat. In verse 31 the disciples wanted Jesus to eat. They had returned with the food. In verse 34, Jesus' answer to eating food was this. His meat or food is to do the will of He that sent Him. We also saw that this woman had tapped into the will of Him that sent her. She had started in the world and was promoted in the church. She was promoted into the *other side* ministry to go outside the walls. She was promoted to an Evangelist to go to the *other side* to evangelize. She was very effective.

Sons are called to eat meat as a part of the *other side* ministry. Babes need meat but will only drink milk. It is hard to swallow the meat of doing the Father's will. The *other side* ministry requires that meat. The Father's will is the meat that gives the *other side* ministers strength and protein. The Father's will is how they receive their nutrition daily for ministry. The Father's will sustain the *other side* ministry. Not their will but the Father's will is done in that *other side* minister's life.

39 And many of Samaritans of the city believed on him for the saying of the woman, which testified, He told me all of ever I did. 40So when the Samarians came unto him they besought him that he would tarry with them; and He abode there 2 days. 41And many more believed because of his word: 42And said unto the woman we believe not because of thy saying: for we have heard him ourselves and know that this is indeed the Christ the Savior of the world. (John 4:39-42) AKJV

God used this woman from the *other side* ministry to change the *other side*. She became focused after her encounter with Jesus. She turns a whole city around for Jesus; spiritual transformed. They received and experienced what she did. People came to Jesus because of her testimony and *other side* ministry. God used this woman with a reputation to confound the wise, to go into the *other side* ministry.

40So when the Samarians came unto him they besought him that he would tarry with them; and He abode there 2 days. 41And many more believed because of his word: 42And said unto the woman we believe not because of thy saying: for we have heard him ourselves and know that this is indeed the Christ the Savior of the world. (John 4:40-42)

Notice they believed from hearing Jesus words, which also confirmed their faith. They did not see, nor ask for signs, miracles or wonders, as the Jews had. These people were affected by what they saw in the woman. After two days with Jesus, the entire town believed. Jesus transformed the woman. She became focused, and ready to finish the work of the *other side* ministry. The woman in turn, engaged these men to become focused to finish the work of the *other side* ministry. They were *all* the *other side* ministers within her womb. In the one seed are the many sons of God waiting to come forth for the *other side* ministry.

9th APPROACH

Overflowing Joy X-Extreme Poverty = A Well of Rich Generosity

Believers in-tuned to spiritual things, usually have no issues giving. They give because they love God and have revelation; He is their primary source. God gives seed to them, the sowers. Therefore, they continually sow, receive seed and reap harvests. Many have experienced severe trials and extreme deep poverty but remain givers. They loved God with all their heart, mind, soul and body. Giving is what they do. They are giving from pure hearts. They give in abundance, no matter what their financial state. When a person gives all they can give, they harness portals from heaven.

They apprehend heaven's proliferation and heaven causes them to give beyond their natural capability. They are giving from pure hearts. Since these factors are in play, God used their giving to become more than they imagined. They apprehend heaven and receive a supernatural well of rich generosity. In II Corinthians 8, Paul became an eyewitness of the harnessed portal from heaven. It was supernaturally flowing into a well of rich generosity.

THE WELL CAUSED THE PEOPLE TO GIVE BEYOND THEIR NATURAL ABILITY

Their hearts were in love with Jesus. They loved the work of the LORD and pleaded to share to enhance the churches. God blew upon their extreme deep poverty.

1Moreover, brethren, we do you to wit of the grace of God bestowed on the churches of Macedonia (from God); 2How that in a grant, donation great trial of affliction the abundance of their joy and their deep poverty abounded unto the riches of their liberality. 3For to their power (what they could give),I bear record (witness),yea, 4And beyond their power (not natural but supernatural giving). 5And this they did, not as we hoped, but first gave their own selves to the lord, and unto us by the will of God!
(2 Corinthians 8:1-5) KJV

1And now, brothers, we want you to know about the grace that God has given the Macedonian churches. 2Out of the most severe trial, their overflowing joy and their extreme poverty welled up in rich generosity. 3for I testify that they gave as much as they were able, and even beyond their ability. Entirely on their own, 4they urgently pleaded with us for the privilege of sharing in this service to the saints." And they exceeded our expectations. 5They gave themselves, to the LORD and then by the will of God to us also.
(2 Corinthians 8:1-5) NIV

In II Kings 4, there is an example of a focused woman. This is symbolic of us, the church. She gives out of her wealth. She harnessed power and grace to give. She then gave to the prophet. In fact, out of her most severe trial, she became a giver. Her most severe trial was the inability to bear a child. Her overflowing joy and extreme poverty gushed up into a well of rich generosity. She gave beyond her ability and upon her own accord.

First, she gave as much as she was able

That was her power and capability. After that, she tapped into heaven's portal and gave beyond her power or capability. It is multiplication; overflowing joy x extreme poverty = a supernatural well of rich generosity. She harnessed a supernatural well that never stops flowing. She also apprehended a supernatural supply proliferation from heaven's portal. This happened because she gave what she could, and God supernaturally augmented it.

8And it fell on a day, that Elisha passed to Shunem, where was a great woman; and she constrained him to eat bread (she is giving). *And so it was, that as oft as he passed by, he turned in thither to eat bread* (she is giving). *9And she said unto her husband, behold now, I perceive that this is an holy man of God, which passeth by us continually. 10Let us make a little chamber* (she is giving), *I pray thee, on the wall; and let us set for him there a bed* (she is giving), *and a table* (she is giving), *and a stool* (she is giving), *and a candlestick* (she is giving) *and it shall be, when he cometh to us, that he shall turn in thither* (she is giving).
(2 Kings 4:8-10) KJV

Giving to Elisha was rewarding to this wealthy woman. She thought of more ways to give to him. She was impressed and perceived that he was a holy man of God. The wealthy woman went over and beyond normal hospitality. She operated in the ministry gift of hospitality. Her focus was serving the guest only, not entertaining. Being hospitable is different from entertainment. Entertainment is about the one hosting the event. Scripture said she was a great woman. Great means she was a woman of power, character, hospitality, riches, grace, prominence, faithfulness and influence. She had a creditable reputation and could be counted on. She was known in her community because of their wealth.

SHE IS GIVING

The giving started on the day she pressed Elisha, the traveling prophet to come to her home for a meal.

SHE IS GIVING

The prophet was made to feel welcome and encouraged by her hospitality, so he decided to accept her offer. After that day, whenever he came to the city, her house was a regular stop for him to eat.

SHE CONTINUES TO GIVE

Though she gave a lot, she felt it was not enough giving. She wanted to bless him more. She spoke with her spouse about it, which reveals that he too was a giver. In her giving she spoke of building a room for the prophet.

He would be able to come and relax there. The room addition would cost a substantial amount of money. Let's look at some of the ways she gives unto the prophet.

SHE IS GIVING

- She purchased the materials.
- She paid the workers for labor.
- In the room she needed a table for him to not only eat his food, but also to write upon, to read and store his books. It will need a linen cloth, dishes and herbs for him to eat.
- She furnished the room with a bed and nice linen that he might rest or stay all night as he pleases.
- She furnished the room with a chair, in which he may sit at the table or just relax.
- She furnished the room with a candle, so he may have the pleasure of night-light to read and see.
- She would have to give him food and drink each time he stays.
- She would have to keep the place clean.
- She keeps the yard in immaculate shape.

When she gives it provides the prophet with a place away from others, where he is free from the noise and distraction of the servants or her family. He would be able to concentrate on prayer, reading, meditation, study and duties of a holy man of God. She wanted his stay to be as pleasant and peaceful as he needed it to be. Therefore, she prepared a room for him to use whenever he was in town. She had a kind, willing and giving heart that gave itself to God first. She had no selfish motives behind what she did. She saw a need and met the need.

11And it fell on a day that he came thither and he turned into the chamber and lay there. 12And he said to Gehazi his servant, call this Shunammite. And when he had called her, she stood before him. 13And he said unto him, Say now unto her, Behold, thou hast been careful for us with all this care; what is to be done for thee? wouldest thou be spoken for to the king, or to the captain of the host? And she answered, I dwell among mine own people. 14And he said, what then is to be done for her? And Gehazi answered, verily she hath no child and her husband is old. 15And he said, call her. And when he had called her, she stood in the door. 16And he said, about this season, according to the time of life, thou shalt embrace a son. And she said, Nay, my lord, thou man of God, do not lie unto thine handmaid.
(2 Kings 4:11-16) KJV

One day, as the prophet laid in his chamber resting, a thought from God came to him. He said to Gehazi, his armor bearer; "Call the Shunamite woman. Tell her I desire to speak with her." When Gehazi called her, she stood before Elisha at the door of the bedchamber. She refused to go any closer because of respect, reverence and humility for the man of God. She waited for him to speak.

He basically asked her what she wanted in exchanged for her kindness. He was asking her what she wanted for giving, caring and her generosity to him. What kind of harvest did she want for the favor she gave to him in providing the room? In other words, he wanted to know what she wanted God to do in her life. The man of God appreciated all she and her husband had given them. He basically asks her, "What can we do for you? What kind of harvest do you want for sowing seed? What kind of harvest do you want for caring? What kind of harvest do you want for your generosity? I want to bestow favor upon you. You have made room for God to move in your life. What prophetic reward would you like? Do you need us to speak to the king or the general about something?" The Word of God said, "The heart of the king (authority) is in God's hand. God can turn His heart for her. Where the word of the king is, there is power."

Instead, she did not take advantage of this time for greed. She said, "My family takes good care of me. We have no needs." She was content and satisfied with her life, family, friends and neighbors. She had neither desire, nor a need to elevate to a higher rank in life. Her husband did not desire to be recognized or honored. She had nothing to settle with the king or general. She had no complaints, nor expected any reward in exchange for her giving.

THE WOMAN DID NOT KNOW IT BUT SHE HAD HARNESSED A SUPERNATURAL SUPPLY PORTAL FROM HEAVEN

This happened due to her giving out of her poverty. This was an overflowing manifestation of her prosperity. She was already prosperous, but her overflow season is upon her. This is the open portal and opportunity for her to receive anything that was delayed. However, she wanted nothing. She was wealthy and felt all her needs were supplied. But, I wondered, "what about her wants"? Was there something she really wanted? Could there have been a secret desire in her heart that she did not talk about? Could she have been giving out of her overflowing joy multiplied by her deep extreme poverty? Could she have been giving to make up for the extreme poverty, and lack of not having a child? If she had a child, she could give the love and gifts to him.

After she refused, the man of God asked his servant Gehazi what they could do for the woman. The servant may have heard talk in the community about the woman. Gehazi informed the prophet, that she had no son and her husband was old. She was not likely to ever bear a child. In bible days, sons were everything. They took care of their parents when they were old, kept the family going, maintained the property and the family inheritance. The belief during bible days was that a life without a son was a life that was incomplete. Being without a child was a great burden for a couple. Children were considered a blessing from God.

The man of God called the woman back into the room. He moved out according to the impression of the Spirit of God upon his spirit. God told Elisha, giving her a son would be the thing to do for her. When the prophet called her a second time, she stood in the door out of reverence and respect for him. Elisha was saying,

"You have blessed the prophet in the name of the prophet; receive your prophetic reward." He declared the Word of the LORD over her life, and promised her that by this time next year, she would have a son. God did nothing in the land, unless he first showed it to his servant the prophet. The prophet saw it; it will be done.

At the announcement of this promise from God, the woman said, "My lord, please do not lie to me." In other words, "Please don't play games or tease me." This statement allows heart exposure. It expressed her anxiety about setting high hopes for a son, and her hopes crumbled. For years, she had accepted being childless as her lot in life. She had not complained but became content and joyful in serving the LORD. She only questioned, because the prophet words provoked her response. He had rocked her undisturbed world. She found it difficult to grasp the joy and hope she felt. But fear and disappointment had become familiar to her. Her issue of never having a child had been settled years ago. She had designed and accepted her life without a child. She feared, if she now accepts this truth or expectation of a son, she would be susceptible to pain, pressure, suffering, agony and sorrow.

17 And the women conceived, and bare a son at that season that Elisha had said unto her, according to the time of life. 18 And when the child was grown, it fell on a day that he went out to his father to the reapers. 19 And he said unto his father, My head, my head. And he said to a lad, carry him to his mother. 20 And when he had taken him and brought him to his mother, he sat on her knees till noon and then died. 21 And she went up and laid him on the bed of the man of God, and shut the door upon him, and went out. (2 Kings 4:17-21) KJV

Here is a wealthy woman. Though wealthy, she most gladly rejoiced in her weaknesses, infirmity, frailties and baroness. She had a thorn in her flesh; she could not conceive. She may have prayed for a child on many occasions, as Hannah did. She may have soon recognized the baroness as a gift. If so, she stopped the complaining, began to appreciate and embraced it as a gift. She believed that she should give herself first to God, which was as much as she had. She gave what she could give; which was of her wealth. She gave according to her power and capability to give. Yet, she gave over and beyond her power to give.

It was a supernatural portal because her heart was willing to give. She gave to God out of her overflowing joy multiplied by her deep extreme poverty (no child), which equals a supernatural well of rich generosity. It was a supernatural manifestation flowing from the portal of heaven. She harnessed a power beyond her power to rejuvenate her husband's body. She had harnessed a power beyond her power to conceive. She harnessed a power beyond her power to birth a son. Her gift of barrenness was so the Father can be glorified in her the son of God. This was not because she or her parents had sinned. It was so she could have access to the supernatural supply portal and proliferation from heaven. She received a son from her own womb.

The child had grown to the age of 6 or 7 years. One day, he went out to the cornfield where his father was. The father was directing the work of the field. After the child had been out in the field with the father for a while, he complained of pain in his head. The pain was so exceedingly great that the little boy repeated himself on how much it hurts. He said, "My head, my head." The father instructed someone to take him to the mom. She may give him medicine to make him well. She would know what to do.

I believe out of her deep, deep love and affection for her only son, she fell to her knees. She laid his head in her bosom to soothe the pain. Her bosom had comforted him in times past of hungry, sickness or injury. This same bosom will comfort him until he awakens. As she held him in her lap, I imagined she prayed over him. She would not give up on her child, no matter what it looked like, in the natural. She would wage a good spiritual warfare over the prophetic word, of a promised son, spoken to her. She believed that with God, all things are possible. God would perfect that that concerned her. Her son concerned her. The boy remained in the position of his mother's arms until he died around noon. She went up to the prophet's chamber and laid him on the bed of the prophet.

I imagined, this woman meditated on the story of this man of God's mentor. Elisha had received a double portion of what was upon his spiritual father. It does rest upon Elisha. Elijah raised the widow of Zarephath's son. In that story, the son was laid upon the prophet's

bed. She believed the same would be done here. Laying him in the prophet's chambers would conceal the news. She could hide the death from the husband, family and friends. She closed the door to prevent vultures from devouring her son's body. Closing the door was a prophetic act. His face, body and skin will not become torn or mutilated. After all, once he woke up, he had to look presentable. This scripture reveals that **the supernatural manifestation from the well of rich generosity seemed to have dried up or died.**
II Kings 4:20 NKJV states, "And when he had taken him and brought him to his mother, he sat on her knees till noon and then died."

22And she called unto her husband and said, Send me, I pray thee, one of the young men & one of the asses, that I may run to the man of God and come again. 23And he said, wherefore wilt thou go to him to day? it is neither new moon, nor sabbath. And she said, it shall be well. 24Then she saddled an ass and said to her servant, Drive and go forward; slack not thy riding for me, except I bid thee.   (2 Kings 4:22-24) KJV

She called her husband and asked him to send a young man and donkey. She wanted to go and visit the man of God and return home. Notice that she did not say one time that the boy was dead. Her husband questioned why she needed to see the man of God. He knew they would see him on the Holy Day. It had not been a month since they had seen him.

She responded to her husband's statements and said,

"IT SHALL BE WELL"

When she responded to him with the words, *"it shall be well"*, she indicated that, it shall be well! These were prophetic words indicating the well will never dry up. Her son had come from the spiritual well of rich generosity from heaven's portal. *It shall be well, with the well.* The well is still flowing, even though it looks, as if it was not, in the natural. Without further words, she was thinking, "please trust me. I am making a decision that will be a well for you, it will be a well for me, and it will be a well for the family." She was calling those things that be not, as though they were. The servant saddled the donkey. She told him, "Go full speed ahead; do not turn to the left or right. Do not look back. Go as fast as you can. Go until I tell you otherwise. Keep the pace."

The woman kept on giving, even though she was in extreme deep poverty. She was experiencing the death of her son, but she had overflowing joy, because she loved God. Giving was her lifestyle. In her giving, she saddled

a donkey for the prophet to return. After all, she was in a hurry, why not ride the donkey? Her resolve is that she saddled the donkey for the man of God; that settles it. She told her servant not to press her to ride the donkey, unless she calls him.

25So she went and came unto the man of God to mount Carmel. And it came to pass, when the man of God saw her afar off, that he said to Gehazi his servant, Behold, yonder is that Shunammite:

26Run now, I pray thee, to meet her and say unto her, is it well with thee? is it well with thy husband? is it well with the child.
(2 Kings 4:25-26) KJV

AND SHE ANSWERED, *"IT IS WELL"*

Are you all still flowing from the supernatural well of rich generosity or has something happened to the well? And she answered, *"It is well"*. She is snared by what she says; therefore, the portal well of rich generosity is still flowing.

27And when she came to the man of God to the hill, she caught him by the feet: but Gehazi came near to thrust her away. And the man of God said, Let her alone; for her soul is vexed within her: and the lord hath hid it from me, and hath not told me. 28Then she said, did I desire a son of my lord? Did I not say, do not deceive me? 29Then he said to Gehazi, Gird up thy loins & take my staff in thine hand and go thy way: if thou meet any man, salute him not and if any salute thee, answer him not again and lay my staff upon the face of the child. 30 And the mother of the child said, As the Lord liveth, I will not leave thee. And he arose, and followed her.   (2 Kings 4:27-30) KJV

The woman arrived where the man of God was teaching the prophets. Elisha saw her from afar. He mentions to his armor bearer that the Shunamite woman was coming. He told Gehazzi to go and meet her and find out why she came. Ask her is it well with her, the husband and the child? In other words, are they still flowing?

The woman answered the prophet's questions. She told Gehazi, "It was well because with God all things are possible. Her well was still flowing, no matter what it looked like in the natural realm. Heaven's supernatural supply never dries up. Satan uses schemes, strategies and methodologies to try to get us to doubt God. He tries to make us think our well is dried up. This woman believed that God raised many from the dead; He can also raise her son. She had harnessed a portal with a supernatural supply from heaven. Despite her natural experience, her supernatural spiritual bank account continued flowing. She had a Word from the LORD about her son, and the Word never returned void.

She responded quickly to the prophet's servant. She did not have time to waste but wanted to see the prophet only. After all, she saw him when he gave her the Word of the LORD. She saw him when he said a child would be born to her. Notice the contrast of position of the woman when she is calm in verses 12, 15. She was different in verse 27, when her soul is vexed; troubled. In verse 12 and 15 Gehazi called her, and she stood before Elisha at the door of the chamber. She refused to go any closer out of great reverence, for the man of God. She waited to hear what he had to say. In verse 27, when she came to Elisha at the hill, she caught him by the feet. In reverence to him, she prostrated herself at his feet. Out of her love and affection for him, she caught hold of his feet. She held onto his feet because her well depended upon it.

Her well would not dry up. Her son had been a

supernatural well of living water, flowing for her and her husband. Her well depended upon it, meant she had prophesied all the way to the man of God. She kept saying, *"It is well, it is well, it is well"*! She was saying, "It Is a Well That Shall Be Well. My son came from the Well." Therefore, her Well depended upon the Well to remain the Well. She was determined not to leave Elisha until he went with her. Gehazi came near to pull her away. She appeared as a troublemaker. The man of God discerned something and said, "Let her alone; her soul is vexed, troubled and bitter." She was so vexed in her spirit that she did not know what else to do.

Elisha mentions a key element. The LORD had hidden the cause and trouble of her pain from him. Prophets are oblivious unless the Lord reveals things to them. The woman asks Elisha questions. She asks, "Did I desire a son of my Lord? Did I not say, do not deceive me, giving me hope of a child? I was satisfied with my life". She answers her own question, by telling the prophet she did not ask for a son. She reminded the prophet; he was the one that told her, she was going to have a son. She probably thought, "It is worst to have a child, and my child is taken from me. If God is going to give me a child, at least let him live. If he is not going to let him live, why trouble me?"

Elisha said to Gehazzi, "Gird up thy loins". That meant that his garment was flowing to the ground. When he girds them up, it will prevent him from falling. It will cause him to travel faster. The prophet was giving instructions that his servant must adhere to. "Do not stop or speak or hold a conversation with anyone. Do not turn to the left or the right. Set your face as a flint and go forward. Hurry, because Satan is trying to prevent the continuous flow of the supernatural well of rich generosity. He is trying to impede the supernatural supply and prosperity in the life of this Shunamite woman. Take my staff and lay it upon the child's face until I get there".

30 And the mother of the child said, As the Lord liveth, and as thy soul liveth, I will not leave thee. And he arose, and followed her. 31 And Gehazi passed on before them & laid the staff upon the face of the child; but there was neither voice, nor hearing. Wherefore he went again to meet him and told him, saying, the child is not awaked. 32 And when Elisha was come into the house, behold, the child was dead and laid upon his bed. 33 He went in therefore, and shut the door upon them twain, and prayed unto the Lord. 34 And he went up, and lay upon the child, and put his mouth upon his mouth, and his eyes upon his eyes, and his hands upon his hands: and stretched himself upon the child; and the flesh of the child waxed warm.

35 Then he returned, and walked in the house to and fro; and went up, and stretched himself upon him: and the child sneezed seven times, and the child opened his eyes. 36 And he called Gehazi, and said, Call this Shunamite. So he called her. And when she was come in unto him, he said, take up thy son. 37 Then she went in, and fell at his feet, and bowed herself to the ground, and took up her son, and went out. (2 Kings 4:30-37) KJV

The woman said, "As the Lord lives and as thy soul

live, I will not leave thee." She was also saying, "I have no faith in your servant and will not go with him. You go and I will not leave you." This woman discerned that Gehazi did not click with Elisha, his master. Elisha went with the woman. Gehazi went on before them. Once he arrived to the woman's house, he laid the staff upon the face of the child as the prophet instructed, but nothing happened. He did not see or feel any signs of life from the child. He left the child and met Elisha informing him the child would not awake.

    Usually a mentee can walk in the same type anointing as his master. They do what their leader does, but Gehazzi could not. He could not perform the miracle his master had performed. Was it because his heart was so far from Elisha? He went behind his master's back and usurped authority. He betrayed Elisha for money as Judas betrayed Jesus for money. In II Kings 5 Gehazzi mentions Elisha was too easy on Naaman. Therefore, he decided to go after Naaman to obtain the money his master refused. Elisha wanted nothing from Naaman for the healing from leprosy. Once Gehazzi reached Naaman, he lied saying Elisha had sent him. He also lied about students in the School of the Prophets needing clothing and money. He took the silver and clothing from Naaman and hid them inside the house. Once he saw Elisha, he was asked where had he been? Gehazzi lied answering, "thy servant went nowhere". Elisha said, "I was there in spirit when Naaaman met you at the chariot. Was not my heart with you? Did you and I not have sweet fellowship? Are you and I not joined to one another? Are you and I not one? Because you have done this, the leprosy that Naaman was cleansed from, will come upon you and your descendants forever." Gehazzi was covered as white as snow. He had accompanied his master for a long time but had not the father son relationship; he had with his master, Elijah.

When they arrived, the child was still on the prophet's bed dead. Elisha went in and shut the door. It was only he and the child. He wanted no one to interrupt his prayers, see the gestures or the posture he used. He prayed to the LORD to restore the child's life. He lay upon the child, as Elijah did lie upon the widow's son at Zarephath in 1 Kings 17. He put his mouth upon his mouth. He put his eyes upon his eyes. He put his hands upon his hands. He stretched himself upon the child. The flesh of the child waxed warm from life, being infused into his body from God. His joints received supply. It is that same supernatural continuous supply from heaven. It is that extreme deep poverty that turned into a well of rich generosity flowing. God sent life and that life more abundantly. Every body part was totally infused; nothing broken and nothing missing.

He left the bedchamber, walked to and fro in deep thought. He had an overwhelming desire for the child's life to be completed. Therefore, he went back to the bedchamber up to the bed. He stretched himself upon the boy, as he did before. He was persistent and relentless. He implored God just as vigorously as the woman that kept troubling the judge until he granted her request. The child sneezed seven times, God's number, the number of completion. A sneeze is the sign of life. Seven sneezes are the sign of Divine Life. This child had received the breath of life. The child's head became clear. Not only was his head clear, but also everyone involved head was clear concerning this episode. Whatever, happened in the head, that manifested itself to destroy the body is cleared. Remember the little boy complained of his head.

Elisha informed Gehazi to call the Shunamite woman to the bedchamber. Once she arrived she took him in her arms as she had done earlier. He was alive, safe and sound. What the enemy meant for evil, God turned it around for good. This was a master deception of Satan. It appeared as if her Supernatural well of rich generosity was over! It appeared as if her supernatural portal supply had stopped flowing. It appeared as if it was gone forever or dead. But, it was just a clog in the passageway that temporarily slowed down supernatural flow.

1Elisha had told the woman whose son he had brought back to life, "Take your family and move to some other place, for the Lord has called for a famine on Israel that will last for seven years." 2So the woman did as the man of God instructed. She took her family and settled in the land of the Philistines for seven years .3After the famine ended she returned from the land of the Philistines, and she went to see the king about getting back her house and land. 4As she came in, the king was talking with Gehazi, the servant of the man of God. The king had just said, "Tell me some stories about the great things Elisha has done."

5 And Gehazi was telling the king about the time Elisha had brought a boy back to life. At that very moment, the mother of the boy walked in to make her appeal to the king about her house and land. "Look, my lord the king!" Gehazi exclaimed. "Here is the woman now, and this is her son—the very one Elisha brought back to life!" 6 "Is this true?" the king asked her. And she told him the story. So he directed one of his officials to see that everything she had lost was restored to her, including the value of any crops that had been harvested during her absence.
(II Kings 8:1-6) NLT

Let us look at another supernatural well of rich generosity manifestation that kept on giving

The woman's generosity worked out in the long run. Her gifts to God were initially just meals for Elijah. Later she built and furnished a small room for the prophet. When she gave, it was given back to her. God's gifts to her included the birth of a son, the resurrection of her son, and warning of a seven-year famine. After the seven-year famine ended, God ensured she would receive her land back, plus seven years of income. Those who refuse to focus on the heart of giving have no seed to sow. A supernatural well of rich generosity that never stopped flowing is what the Shunammite woman harnessed because she just kept giving.

For example, Paul was provoked to focus

At times God will provoke us to focus. Giving self as a minister is born from our lack of strength or weakness. Therefore, we can harness a power available to us for strength. God taught Apostle Paul to learn contentment in any state. Whatever state he was in, he learned to give. When called into ministry, whatever is going on in our daily lives to buffet us is sufficient. Paul is taught to give even in times of weakness. God is powerful during that time of weakness in his life. Therefore, as the woman gave out of her wealth, God tells Paul to give out of his lack or weakness. He is to give; minister the word, build churches, perform signs, miracles and wonders.

Notice how Apostle Paul apprehended the well of supernatural rich generosity. He was also in deep extreme poverty, which was a thorn in his flesh. He prayed for God to remove what he called a thorn in the flesh. But God revealed to Paul, whom receive many revelations, the plans God had for him. God told Paul that His grace was sufficient for him. His power would manifest when Paul was weak. Knowing that, Paul decided to glory or become excited in weakness. Paul's confidence in weakness led him to become focused. Therefore, the Apostle's Overflowing Joy X-Extreme Deep Poverty welled up into a Well of Supernatural Rich Generosity.

7 And lest I should be exalted above measure through the abundance of the revelations, there was given to me a thorn in the flesh, the messenger of Satan to buffet me, lest I should be exalted

above measure. 8For this thing I besought the Lord thrice, that it might depart from me. 9And he said unto me, My grace is sufficient for thee: for my strength is made perfect in weakness. Most gladly therefore will I rather glory in my infirmities, that the power of Christ may rest upon me. 10Therefore I take pleasure in infirmities, in reproaches, in necessities, in persecutions, in distresses for Christ's sake: for when I am weak, then am I strong.
(II Corn 12:7-10) KJV

    This paragraph is the Message bible version in summary on II *Corinthians 12:7-10*. Because of the extravagance of those revelations, gifts, callings, mysteries, supply etc. and so, I wouldn't get a big head; I was given the gift of a handicap to keep me in constant touch with my limitations. The handicap is a boundary that prevents me from going beyond my measure of authority. Satan's angel did his best to get me down; what he in fact did was push me to my knees. No danger of walking around high and mighty. At first, I did not think of it as a gift and begged God to remove it. This was the gift of grace. It was a gift of power beyond my natural capability. Three times I did that, and then God told me, "My Grace was enough; it's all you needed. My strength comes into its own fruition in your weakness. My strength is executed when you are weak." Once Paul heard that, he was glad to let it happen. He quit focusing on the handicap and began appreciating the gift. It was a case of Christ's strength moving in on his weakness. It is Christ' supernatural power moving in on his natural power. He believes and now he takes limitations in stride. A limitation tries to cut him down to size. Therefore, abuse, accidents, opposition and bad breaks; whatever; he just let Christ take over. The weaker he gets, the stronger he becomes.

God opened the heaven and answered Paul's prayer. The prayer was not answered in the way Paul hoped. God basically told Paul, the thorn was going to remain in his life. God gave Paul what he really needed. He gave him the capability to tolerate the thorn. Paul was becoming acquainted with God's sufficient grace through this thorn. From God's view, the thorn caused Paul to apprehend a power from heaven that was always available to him.

There is a generosity and kindness God displays to Paul in his weakness. It was from a well of supernatural rich generosity. This well flows especially in areas of lack. This well flows in areas where weakness becomes strength. This well flows in areas where lack becomes wealth. This well flows in areas where nothing becomes something. This well flows in areas where poor become rich. This well flows in areas where turmoil becomes peace.

Paul asked God to remove the thorns three times. The thorn was debilitating and a hindrance. But God said, "My grace is sufficient for you". God decides since Paul will teach the word of God without compromise, he needs a buffer. If Paul wanted the power to rest upon him, he had to remain weak. If Paul wanted the anointing to accompany his preaching, he had to remain weak. When Paul was weak, only then was God, strong in his life. In order to prevent Paul from becoming caught up in his own greatness, God allowed the thorn. A thorn given to him was designed to buffer and safeguard him from his flesh. It was there to defend the spiritual things of God.

God's grace and power enabled him to bear, and take pleasure in infirmities, in reproaches, in necessities, in persecutions, in distresses for Christ's sake. Paul seem delighted to go through various troubles and suffering to apprehend that supernatural well of rich generosity. God's strength and power was made perfect, complete and fulfilled in Paul. His strength became God's strength manifested within. Paul received grace in character, humility, and the capability to empathize with others.

When we are strong in our own abilities, resources and skills, we tend to leave God out. It can lead us to pride. When we are weak, we allow God to fill us with His power. When obstacles come, we depend upon God. There is power outside our power to assist us in our personal life and in ministry. Paul apprehended this power from above. This power gave him capability to give and move out into ministry. That is why Paul can say in I Corinthians 2:4-5,

4And my speech and my preaching was not with enticing words of man's wisdom, but in demonstration of the Spirit and of power: 5That your faith should not stand in the wisdom of men, but in the power of God.   (I Corinthians 2:4-5) KJV

Grace was the power that caused Paul to move in ministry of excellence

He lived under a supernatural open heaven portal to receive. This power Paul apprehended caused him to do what he does. This power caused Paul to talk the way he talked, to walk the walk he preached about, and enable Paul to love the churches the way he loved them. Paul could endure prison as he did. This power caused Paul to shake the snake off him and suffer no harm. This power allowed Paul to know Christ in the resurrection of His power and the fellowship of His suffering. This power caused Paul to bear burdens of the churches daily, to walk in the apostolic, to become abased and to become abound. This power caused Paul to come to visions and revelations of the Lord, to know a man in Christ above fourteen years, whether he was in and out of his body and could not tell, God knew. This power caused Paul to be one caught up to the third heaven, to become caught up into paradise and hear unspeakable words, which it is not lawful for a man to utter. This power caused Paul to be an apostle not of men or by man, but by Christ and God the Father, who raised him from the dead. This power caused Paul to wrought special miracles by his hands. This power caused Paul's handkerchief from his body lay upon the sick and the diseased whereby evil spirits departed from them.

Power and Grace in God confirms we have done all we know to do; it says still stand

We have in times past done things in our capability and power. After we finish, God allows us to apprehend power above our power. It opens a well of supernatural rich generosity. Therefore, we can deal with anything. Therefore, this bears repeating from the opening of this chapter. Believer's in-tuned to spiritual things, have no issues giving. They give because they love God and know that He is their primary Source. They walk in the revelation that God gives seed to the sower. Therefore, they continually sow, receive seed and reap harvests. Many believers experience severe trials and extreme deep poverty but remain givers. They love God with all their heart, mind, soul and body; giving is what they do. They give in abundance no matter what their financial state. Severe trials or suffering lack does not change the amount they sow. When a person gives all they have, and hold nothing back, they harness the portal from heaven.

    They apprehend heaven's proliferation and heaven cause them to give beyond their natural capability. They are giving from a truthful and pure heart. Since these factors are in play, God used their giving to become more than they imagined. They apprehend heaven and receive a supernatural well of rich generosity. In II Corinthians 8 Paul became an eyewitness of the harnessed portal from heaven. It was supernaturally flowing into a well of rich generosity. That well caused the people to give beyond their natural ability. Their hearts were in love with Jesus. They loved the work of the Lord and pleaded to share to enhance the churches. God blew upon their extreme deep poverty.

10th APPROACH

An Uncontrolled Fire Becomes A Controlled Fire

When we are tested in fire, some of us will conform, some of us will inform, and some of us will transform. Unprescribe means not set, not agreed upon, not given, not prearranged, not approved, not recommended and not advised. Prescribes means set, agreed, given, prearranged, approved, recommended and advised. Uncontrolled means out of controlled, not regulated, out of order, deviation from the original, undisciplined, non-compliant, and not submissive. Controlled means govern, guide, regulate, compliant, discipline or submitted.

If a person is taking blood pressure medications and their blood pressure increases or is out of control, it may be due to non-compliant, to a diet, exercise and medications. They have caused this effect.

There are fires in many of our lives out of controlled, due to sparks we caused, others caused, and God allowed them to remain. God allowed these fires to continue, because it gives Him opportunity to control uncontrolled fires.

THE FIRE

1 Peter 1:6–7 NABRE, "Now for a little while you may have to suffer various trials, so that the genuineness of your faith, more precious than gold, which though perishable is tested by fire, may rebound (prove to be genuine) to praise and glory & honor at the revelation of Jesus Christ."

Peter wrote to the Christians that were suffering persecution because of their testimony for Christ. He reminds them that they could have joy in sorrow. They could also have joy in the knowledge that various trials were only for a season or a little while; whereas the glory will be forever. Their suffering is for a purpose and they in turn will bear much fruit.

Our faith is tested with a type fire that purifies gold

Gold is a symbol of beauty and value. Gold is tested by fire in a refining method. It was used in ancient times. The craftsmen would sit next to fire as it is heated. The temperature was usually 1,947 degrees. This equals 21 which added together; God's number; which means, God controls the fire. The craftsmen skim the dross from the top as the heat pushes the dross up. All the impurities are seen as it comes up and out of the gold. Only then does gold take on a higher value.

Peter went on to say that our faith is more precious than gold. The genuineness of faith from being tested is more valuable than gold. Genuine character comes out of tests! The real us appears when we are tested. The pressure and heat from the refiner's fire pushes the dross up out of our lives to reveal impurities. It is the filthiness of flesh and spirit. Flesh is our outward life. The spirit is our inward life (character, integrity, why we do what we do). Once the impurities are skimmed off of us, we take on a higher value.

Peter proves this by contrasting our faith with gold. Our faith value is more precious and valuable than gold. Of all the substances known to man, gold is one of the most imperishable. It can be subjected to intense heat and might seem to be indestructible. But the truth is that gold perish through use, pressure, fire and become lost. Men take great efforts to test gold, just to prove it contains no dross. It's our faith, not gold God will display as evidence of His victory.

ONE TEST IS NOT ENOUGH FOR GENUINE FAITH

That is why Peter used the word various trials. We will encounter all type or various trials just to ensure we are valuable. There is joy lurking in our future when we are tested in many trials. Various trials reveal different depths of our character. A trial will reveal our character in finances when income tax time comes; will we give to God; will we lie on taxes to get more. Marriage trial reveals a different depth in character than a trial with the children; cheating or truancy from school. Various trials can be with our finances, children, family, faith, education, friends, occupation, patience, love, singleness, marriage, etc. We only suffer for a little while. But trials display character and genuine faith.

The time will come for inspection and Jesus will "find" if tests were sufficient. Will He find true faith? True faith is indestructible. When we go through several severe trials and test, instead of our faith becoming destroyed, we use it as momentum and build upon that faith. That indestructible faith becomes the nourishment we need to feed upon. Jesus then find us purer than gold. Job proved this in Job 13:15 after his heavy loses. He said, "Though He slay me, yet will I trust Him". The three Hebrew men in the Babylonian furnace were literally tested by fire. The fire proved their faith to be real and indestructible.

The genuineness of faith can be proven only by fire. Genuine faith will result in bringing praise, glory and honor to God. This means God will reward every instance of our faith that stood the test. God will praise those that are joyful when trouble surrounds. He will reward glory and honor to those that accept the trials as confidence in Him. We must accept trials as God's refining process to burn away impurities. As gold is heated and the impurities float to the top and skimmed off to be used, so it is with us. We are heated from test, so impurities come out, and God uses us.

My brethren, count it all joy when ye fall into divers temptations; Knowing this, that the trying of your faith worketh patience. But let patience have her perfect work, that ye may be perfect and entire, wanting nothing.   (James 1:2-4) KJV

Consider it a sheer gift, friends, when tests and challenges come at you from all sides. You know that under pressure, your faith-life is forced into the open and shows its true colors. So don't try to get out of anything prematurely. Let it do its work so you become mature and well developed, not deficient in any way.

(James 1:2–4) MSG

When trouble comes our way, it is an opportunity to count it for great joy. We know when our faith is tested; God is saying, "It is time to grow. Just grow instead of complaining. When our patience is fully developed, we will be perfect and complete, needing nothing. If we need anything our patience is not fully developed. James does not say *if* trouble comes our way, but *when* trouble comes our way. Trouble is coming. We will never get away from trouble. When they come means they are inevitable. Sometimes they come as drips and other times as floods. Don't rebel, don't faint and don't quit but rejoice and count them. These problems are not enemies bent on destroying us. Tests are friends that have come to assist us in developing Christian character. We have trouble, but it is for us to profit. Turn trials into lessons. In tough times we learn patient and steadfastness.

Various trials reveal the depth of our character

God is producing Christlikeness in each of us. We do well and be kind when things are going well, but what about when our back is against the wall and pressure is on? Scripture remind us,

21 Because that, when they knew God, they glorified him not as God, neither were thankful; but became vain in their imaginations, and their foolish heart was darkened. 22 Professing themselves to be wise, they became fools, 23 And changed the glory of the uncorruptible God into an image made like to corruptible man, a nd to birds, and fourfooted beasts, and creeping things.
(Romans 1:21-23) KJV

    In this scripture, they were thinking foolish ideas about what God was like. Thinking these foolish ideas darkened and confused their mind. They lost their capacity to see and think clearly. They claimed to be wise but were fools. Instead of worshipping God, they worshipped the creatures God made. They gave themselves over to speculations about other gods. They grew more conceited over their self-knowledge and plunged deeper into ignorance and nonsense.

    Man is instinctively religious. He must have some object of worship. When he refuses to worship the living God, he made his own gods of wood, stone, representing snakes, birds, animals, man and creeping things. Notice the downward progression of man to birds, to animals to snakes or creeping things.

    He will soon become like these things he worships. If he worships the snake, he will soon degrade to live as free as he pleases. As his concept of God degenerates, his morals degenerate as well. A worshipper generally considers himself inferior to his object of worship. Man will worship creatures if he does not worship the Creator. Man was created to worship God. Whatever we define as our god, we will worship. We make gods out of people, jobs, titles, children, spouses, pride, houses, possessions, money etc. God clearly says we shall have no other god before Him.

No man can serve two masters: for either he will hate the one and love the other; or else he will hold to the one and despise the other. Ye cannot serve God and mammon (treasure, ambition, loot, capital, affluence, greed).   (Matthew 6:24) KJV

We cannot worship two gods at once. We will love one more and hate the other. We will do for one and neglect the other. We will spend time with one and spend no time with the other. We can't worship God and money. In other words, we cannot worship God and worldly influences. Usually our bank accounts transactions reveal whom we worship the most.

Daniel Chapter 3
Conformers are in verses 1-7
They are imitators that agree, follow and obey

1Nebuchadnezzar the king (symbolic of Satan) made an image of gold, whose height was threescore cubits, and the breadth thereof six cubits: he set it up in the plain of Dura, in the province of Babylon. 2Then Nebuchadnezzar the king sent to gather together the princes, the governors and the captains, the judges, the treasurers, the counsellors, the sheriffs and all the rulers of the provinces, to come to the dedication of the image which Nebuchadnezzar the King had set up. 3Then the princes, the governors, and captains,

the judges, the treasurers, the counselors, the sheriffs and all the rulers of the provinces, were gathered together unto the dedication of the image that Nebuchadnezzar the king had set up and they stood before the image that Nebuchadnezzar had set up.
(Daniel 3:1-3) KJV

We see a strategic military operation of the kingdom of darkness setup and implemented. Satan uses flesh and blood to accomplish his task. Though he uses the king, the battle is neither against flesh and blood, nor him. Demons are not flesh and blood, and Satan controls them. They are a powerful demonic force, and their mission is to defeat all that have obtained victory in Christ Jesus. Every device Satan uses, is strategically used, to turn us from God.

For we wrestle not against flesh and blood, but against principalities, against powers, against the rulers of the darkness of this world, against spiritual wickedness in high places.
(Ephesians 6:12) KJV

This fight is against Satan and his angels. Satan strategy is to make images and strong delusions (illusions, misunderstanding and mistakes) to appear real. His method is to exalt his knowledge above the knowledge of God. He wants to exalt his imaginations into our thinking. Therefore, he exalts what he tells and shows us above what God said to us in the Word. Everything Satan does, is done to outdo God.

13For thou hast said in thine heart, I will ascend into heaven, I will exalt my throne above the stars of God: I will sit also upon the mount of the congregation, in the sides of the north. 14I will ascend above the heights of the clouds. I will be like the most High.
(Isaiah 14:13-14) KJV

In Daniel 3:1-3, worshipping other gods and compromising will cause the princes, the governors, and captains, the judges, the treasurers, the counselors, the sheriffs and all the rulers of the provinces, to escape an unprescribed fire. This king made a god out of gold that was 90 feet high and 90 feet wide. He worships it and intends others to worship it. Satan's strategy is to influence those in leadership to follow him. All the officials were ordered to attend this dedication ceremony of the statue. Notice how the king gathered everyone in leadership. Leadership is the authority over groups of people according to their title. Whatever the leaders or examples do, the others will do as well.

Nebuchadnezzar, the king sent for leaders in descending rank. The satraps were the top governors. Next, were the captains, who were secondary rulers. There were chief arbitrators; regional judges. Next, were the masters of treasury, the lawyers of the cabinets and senates, the sheriffs, or law enforcers. Lastly, were all rulers of the jurisdictions that rule anything, too numerous to name. Upon orders from Satan, the king contacted everybody who was anybody to come to the dedication and worship the golden image. He wanted all to be faithful to his cause.

All the important leaders showed up and took their positions

They stood before the stature King Nebuchadnezzar, erected. None of the leaders discerned Satan's tactics and deception. All followed the king's demonic activity. The top leaders became *conformers* to gain favor with the king. In other words, leading politicians were willing to *conform*. They were willing to do whatever it took to get the king's approval. They were categorized as important, but lacked courage to say no. All were willing to *conform* to retain their jobs and positions. All were willingly to *conform* because they showed up to worship an image. All these great leaders escaped the unprescribed fire because they were *conformers*. The leaders were delighted to *conform* to the king's desires, as long as their lives were spared from the unprescribed fire.

4Then an herald cried aloud, To you it is commanded, O people, nations and languages &3that at what time ye hear the sound of the cornet, flute, harp, sackbut, psaltery, dulcimer and all kinds of music, ye fall down and worship the golden image that Nebuchadnezzar the king hath set up. 6And whoso falleth not down and worshippeth shall the same hour be cast into the midst of a burning fiery furnace.7Therefore at that time, when all the people heard the sound of the cornet, flute, harp, sackbut, psaltery and all kinds of musick, all the people, the nations and the languages, fell down and worshipped the golden image that Nebuchadnezzar the king had set up.   *(Daniel 3:4-7) KJV)*

The announcement, "Attention everyone! Every race, color, and creed, listen! When you hear the big band, orchestra begin to play the trumpets, trombones, tubas, baritones, drums and cymbals, fall to your knees and worship the gold statue the king set up. Anyone who does not kneel and worship will instantly be tossed into a roaring furnace." As the orchestra played all the music instruments, every race, color, and creed—fell to his or her knees and worshiped the gold statue.   *(Daniel 3:4-7) MSG*

    There is a sound Satan has for all that will hear him. That sound will cause the worship of other things. His sound will cause us to dance to his demonic activity. His goal is to sound like the voice of God. Satan is a deceiver with many camouflage sounds. He disguises as if he has our best interest at hand. Satan even deceives Eve with a sound that convinces her to doubt God. A good example of his sound is in the Garden of Eden. When God said to Adam and Eve, "If you eat from the tree of the knowledge of good and evil, you would surely die." Satan said to Eve, "God knows you will not die. Matter of fact, God knows that you will be like God." Eve was already like God. Satan is cunning. He plants false thoughts to get what he wants. Actually, he wants to be like God! He parades himself as an angel of light to sound like God. He has a form of godliness to sound like God, but there is no power.

    In Galatians 3, Paul told the Galatians they were foolish. He wanted to know what happened to them. He said, "O foolish Galatians, who have bewitched you?

"Who hypnotized you? Who put a spell upon you? How soon are you pulled away unto *Another Gospel*? After hearing the gospel, how can you go to something that is not the gospel?" Paul was saying in other words, "Whose and what sound are you listening to? What are you hearing?" Satan parades himself as an angel of light. Paul said, "If we or an angel from heaven tells you something other than what God has said in the Word of God, let him be accursed." Satan and his demonic powers are instruments with a sound similar to God. Satan is a Master of Musical sounds. We should not listen nor dance to the demonic sounds of Satan.

There is a different sound for the saints of God. It is a sound that arrives from heaven specifically for them. We can hear the sound of the abundance of rain. We are dry without God. We can hear the sound of the times of refreshing, which comes from the presence of the Lord. We can hear the sound that suddenly comes as a rushing mighty wind and fills our house. We can hear the sound appearing as cloven tongues, like fire that sits upon each of us. We can hear the sound where we are all filled with the Holy Ghost. We can hear the sound when we speak with other tongues, as the Spirit gives us utterance. We can hear the sound of 24 elders worshipping God in Spirit and Truth.

There is also a sound sent from heaven of the voice of His Apostle, Prophet, Evangelist, Pastor and Teacher. He that has an ear, let him hear, what the Spirit is saying unto he, the church, through the sound of these instruments of God. The purpose of His instruments of sound is spoken of in Ephesians 4:10-15.

10He that descended is the same also that ascended up far above all heavens, that he might fill all things. 11And he gave some, apostles and some, prophets and some evangelist, and some, pastors and teachers.12 It is for the perfecting of the saints, for the work of the ministry, for the edifying of the body of Christ.

13 Till we all come in the unity of the faith and of the knowledge of the Son of God, unto a perfect man, unto the measure of the stature of the fullness of Christ. 14That we henceforth be no more children, tossed to and fro, and carried about with every wind of doctrine, by the sleight of men and cunning craftiness, whereby they lie in wait to deceive; 15But speaking the truth in love, may grow up into him in all things, which is the head, even Christ.
(Ephesians 4:10-15) KJV

Satan tried tempting Jesus to worship him, just as he tempted the leaders to worship the image. Jesus refused to adhere to a demonic strategist called Satan. Satan could not do anything or give Jesus anything to worship him. When Jesus went through his wilderness experience, He had God's faith. He chose God's Word over Satan suggestions and strategies. The most important thing about Jesus in the wilderness is that He was able to discern, recognize, perceive and distinguish the sound of Satan from the sound of God.
(1) It was because Jesus was full of the Holy Ghost against Satan's sound.
(2) He is led by the Spirit of God against the sound of

Satan.

(3) He exercised His authority and told the sound of Satan to get behind him.

(4) He knew what was written in the Word of God against the sound of Satan's words.

(5) He knew the sound of the One he served and worshipped verses the sound of Satan's worship and service.

And Jesus being full of the Holy Ghost returned from Jordan and was led by the Spirit into the wilderness. The devil taking Him up into a high mountain, shewed unto Him all the kingdoms of the world in a moment of time. And the devil said unto Him, all this power will I give thee and the glory of them: for that is delivered unto me and to whomsoever I will I give it. If thou therefore wilt worship me, all shall be thine. And Jesus answered and said unto him, Get thee behind me, Satan, for it is written, thou shalt worship the Lord thy God and Him only shalt thou serve.

(Luke 4:1, 5-7)

Informers are found in verses 8-12 The reporters, conversationalist and notifiers

8Wherefore at that time certain Chaldeans came near, and accused the Jews. 9They spake and said to the king Nebuchadnezzar, O king, live forever. 10Thou, O king, hast made a decree, that every man that shall hear the sound of the cornet, flute, harp, sackbut, psaltery, and dulcimer and all kinds of musick, shall fall down and worship the golden image:

11 And whoso falleth not down and worshippeth, that he should be cast into the midst of a burning fiery furnace. There are certain Jews whom thou hast set over the affairs of the province of Babylon, Shadrach, Meshach and Abednego; these men, O king, have not regarded thee: they serve NOT thy gods, nor worship the golden image which thou hast set up. 12 There are certain Jews whom thou hast set over the affairs of the province of Babylon, Shadrach, Meshach, and Abednego; these men, O king, have not regarded thee: they serve not thy gods, nor worship the golden image which thou hast set up. (Daniel 3:8-12, KJV)

THE INFORMERS WILL DO ANYTHING TO ESCAPE A PRESCRIBED FIRE

These are people that flattered the king with compliments about his greatness, power and authority. They used flattery by saying, "O king you are to live forever." These *informers* pretended to be the king's friends. They lied to him. Therefore, they left no stone unturned to kill Shadrach, Meshach and Abednego. The *informers* exaggerated stories about the three young men disrespecting and dishonoring the king. They stepped out of their authority to become district attorneys. They complained that the Jews would not submit to the king.

They reminded the king about the strict orders announced in the decree. They did not want him to forget his warning. He said, "Once the orchestra started to play, whoever did not fall on their knees, worship the image, set up by the king, will be thrown into the inferno. They called the three Hebrew young men by name, Shadrach, Meshach and Abednego. They said, "These offenders did not obey your decree. They are the men, dear king; you placed in high positions of authority. These men are ignoring you. They don't respect your gods. They won't worship the gold statue you erected."

NOTICE HOW THE SCRIPTURE COME TO LIGHT

The scripture speaks of, "Satan as the accuser of the brethren." Revelation 12:10, "And I heard a loud voice saying in heaven, now is come salvation, and strength, and the kingdom of our God, and the power of his Christ: for the accuser of our brethren is cast down, which accused them before our God day and night." This is magnifying that we wrestle not against flesh and blood, but against principalities, against powers, against the rulers of the darkness of this world, against spiritual wickedness in high places; (Ephesians 6:12). If Satan can convince us that people, flesh and blood, is the enemy, he has sold us a counterfeit and a deception. These are the *informers* and the king's favorites. They really wanted the high positions; the king gave the three Jews.

LET US TAKE A DEEPER LOOK INTO THE KINGDOM OF DARKNESS ORCHESTRATED BY SATAN

The strongman is the spirit of jealousy. It dispatches demonic spirits that manifest into murder. Jealousy does not care how it causes others to suffer in their body, soul or mind. Jealousy is cruel, harsh, mean, nasty, evil and relentless. Its mission is seeing its rivalry fall. Jealousy says, "I am hurting because of your success". Jealousy's pride is wounded when someone else is promoted. Jealousy's *informers* will murder others and appear blameless. They disguise and appear blameless. Their goal is to save themselves from an unprescribed and uncontrolled fire. Scripture says, *"We all have sinned and come short of the glory of God." (Romans 3:23)*

In John 18: 15-17, 25-27 (NKJV), there is a mighty man of God, who was an *informer*. He informed people and denied he knew Jesus, to keep from burning in an unprescribed fire. Peter wanted to win the king's favor. He did not want to be imprisoned nor possibly crucified. When we don't want to be crucified, we will conform and *inform*. Even Paul said, "Do not be conformed to this world but be ye transformed by the renewing of your mind."

PETER DENIES JESUS

15 And Simon Peter followed Jesus and so did another disciple. Now that disciple was known to the high priest and went with Jesus into the courtyard of the high priest. 16 But Peter stood at the door outside. Then the other disciple, who was known to the high priest, went out and spoke to her who kept the door and brought Peter in. 17 Then, the servant girl who kept the door said to Peter, "You are not also one of this Man's disciples, are you?" He saith, "I am not".   *(John 18: 15-17) NKJV*

(1) He said or *informed* her saying, "I am not."

PETER DENIES JESUS

Now Simon Peter stood and warmed him. Therefore, they said to him, "You are not also one of His disciples, are you?" He denied it, and said, "I am not".   *(John 18: 25) KJV*

(2) He said or *informed* them saying, "I am not.

PETER DENIES JESUS

One of the servants of the high priest, a relative of him whose ear Peter cut off, said, "Did I not see you in the garden with Him?" Peter then denied again: and immediately the cock crew.
(John 18:26-27) KJV

(3) He said or *informed* the high priest servant by

DENYING JESUS AGAIN

We too become *informers*, when we are unbecoming in our Christian lifestyle and behavior as believers. We inform the world, in an uncontrolled or unprescribed, fire that we have denied Jesus.

TRANSFORMERS FOUND IN VERSES 13-30 ARE MODIFIERS, CHANGERS, CONVERTERS AND MODERNIZERS

13Then Nebuchadnezzar in his rage and fury commanded to bring Shadrach, Meshach, and Abednego. Then they brought these men before the king. 14Nebuchadnezzar spake and said unto them, is it true, O Shadrach, Meshach and Abednego, do not ye serve my gods, nor worship the golden image which I have set up? 15Now if ye be ready that at any time, ye hear the sound of the cornet, flute, harp, sackbut, psaltery and dulcimer and all kinds of musick, ye fall down and worship the image which I have made; well: but if ye worship not, ye shall be cast the same hour into the midst of a burning fiery furnace and who is that God that shall deliver you out of my hands?   (Daniel 3:13-15) KJV

The king was furious and in a rage. The ruler of the world could not rule his own spirit.

He that hath no rule over his own spirit, is like a city that is broken down and without walls. (Proverbs 25:28) KJV

This man cannot control his emotions. He was like a house that is without doors and windows. Therefore, Satan enters and takes over. The man has no defense because he left himself open for the thief or enemy to come in to rule. He has no defense against uncontrolled emotions that destroys his personality. He was hotter than fire because they disobeyed him.

The officials ensured that the young men did not escape punishment. The king demanded the young men show up to give an account of their behavior. He questioned them just to ensure there was no misunderstanding. He was furious, but deep down he wanted to make sure they were guilty of the accusations. In other words, they were valuable administrators, and he did not want to lose them. If the king could, he would probably ask them, "Have you done this impulsively and intentionally? Did you do this out of misinterpretation of my words; if so this can be an acquittal? Is it a joke? Are you seriously not going to worship my gods? Are you mocking me?" He gave them a second chance to get it right. Their refusal caused the king to become defiant and asks, "Who is that God that shall deliver you out of my hands? Let Him do it, if He can." It sounded like the king knew they would be rescued. It sounds like a word of wisdom. The King was saying, "You can either choose death or life; choose to turn or to burn. The choice is yours."

1Now we beseech you, brethren, by the coming of our Lord Jesus Christ, and by our gathering together unto Him, 2That ye be not soon shaken in mind, or be troubled, neither by spirit, nor by word, nor by letter as from us, as that the day of Christ is at hand. 3Let no man deceive you by any means: for that day shall not come, except there come a falling away first and that man of sin be revealed, the son of perdition; 4Who opposeth and exalteth himself above all that is called God, or that is worshipped; so that he as God sitteth in the temple of God, shewing himself that he is God.
II Thessalonians 2:1-4) KJV

I imagine the three Hebrew men heard a sound, but it was not the sound everyone else heard. They heard the sound of the coming of the Lord through the clouds with a shout to rescue them. This is what I call *"the rapture"*. When God come to get us out of something, we have experienced *"the rapture"*. These men knew the law of God regarding graven images and idolatry. It was unacceptable. Therefore, they faced reality of deciding concerning worshipping idols.

This king was setting himself up as though he was God. II Thessalonian 2 says, to not be so soon or quickly trouble or shaken in our mind by this type of deceiving spirit. Do not be alarmed by a word that is spoken or a letter that will say the Lord has come. The king wanted them to worship him as though he was the LORD. The man of perdition opposes and exalts himself above the knowledge of God. He tries to sit upon the throne of our heart as a god.

Daniel 3:15 encourages there is a Coming of the Lord

There will be a Coming of the Lord for these three young men. The King seems to know that. He declared and wanted to know, "Who is that God that shall deliver you out of my hands?"

Many are waiting for Jesus to burst through the sky. I submit unto you that; this Coming has been going on for a long time. Jesus is always Coming to rapture us out of different things. There is a Coming of the Lord when He saved us. There is a Coming of the Lord when we are saved from a car accident. There is a Coming of the

Lord when He heals our body. There is a Coming of the Lord to pay our mortgage. There is a Coming of the Lord when signs, miracles and wonders occur. There is a Coming of the Lord when He leads and guides us into all truth. There is a Coming of the Lord when He is a light unto our feet and a lamp unto our path. There is a Coming of the Lord when we have no food on our table but still eat. There is a Coming of the Lord when He supplies, all our needs according to His riches in glory. There is a Coming of the Lord when we trust in Him with all our heart and lean not unto our own understanding. There is a Coming of the Lord when love is shed abroad in our heart by the Holy Ghost. There is a Coming of the Lord when He gives seed to the sower and bread to the eater. There is a Coming of the Lord when our prayers are answered. There is a Coming of the Lord when we thought we were going to lose our mind and could not. There is a Coming of the Lord when He delivers us from all type addictions. There is a Coming of the Lord to deliver us out of a murder plot. There is a Coming of the Lord to rescue marriages. There is a Coming of the Lord when our child drives beyond the posted speed limit but makes it home safely. There is a Coming of the Lord when the finances cannot make ends meet, but they are met. There is a Coming of the Lord when we have peace that surpasses all our understanding. Jesus is always Coming and always Rapturing. When He always Comes, our eyes definitely see Him! He always Comes and does something to or for us.

16Shadrach, Meshach and Abednego, answered and said to the king, O Nebuchadnezzar, we are not careful to answer thee in this matter. 17 If it be so, our God whom we serve is able to deliver us from the burning fiery furnace and He will deliver us out of thine hand, O king. 18 But if not, be it known unto thee, O king, that we will not serve thy gods, nor worship the golden image which thou hast set up.   (Daniel 3:16-18) KJV

These three young men refused to violate the commandments of God

3Thou shalt have no other gods before me.4Thou shalt not make unto thee any graven image, or any likeness of any thing that is in heaven above, or that is in the earth beneath, or that is in the water under the earth. 5Thou shalt not bow down thyself to them, nor serve them: for I the Lord thy God Am a jealous God, visiting the iniquity of the fathers upon the children unto the third and fourth generation of them that hate me.   (Exodus 20:3-5) KJV

They vowed in their heart never to worship the image. They declared, "Our God, whom we serve, is able to deliver us from the burning fiery furnace. He will also deliver us from your hand. But if not, let it be known to you, O king, that we do not serve your gods, nor will we worship the gold image you set up. If God chose not to deliver us, we shall not worship your image to escape an unprescribed or uncontrolled fire." In other words, they were saying, "We have encountered many trials." They now specialize in unprescribed fires. Unprescribed or uncontrolled fires are really to their advantage.

When the young men said, "But if" that meant they yielded to God's will and God's power. They did not doubt God's ability, but neither did they pretend to know God's Will. Everything done must be done as unto the LORD. I imagined the three young men thought of Job's words 13: 15 and agreed; "Though He slay me, yet will I trust Him." God's thoughts and ways are higher than their thoughts and ways. Were they called as martyrs like Stephen? No matter what happens, they refused to turn their back on God. They were showing the king that they would not serve his gods.

It takes the God kind of faith to have this type courage and boldness. That is their final answer. They needed no defense. God brought them to this faith in Him. They have momentum that was gathered from previous trials. They stood firm then and will stand firm now. They understood that obedience to God is better than sacrifice for man. They refused to conjure up an excuse to compromise. They refused to do as the Romans did because they were in Rome. They refused to follow the crowd or submit to their colleague's peer pressure. They did not yield to Satan's schemes, strategies or methodologies. They were willing to stand-alone with God.

THESE ARE THE *TRANSFORMERS* BECAUSE OF THEIR FAITH OF GOD

The renewing of their mind through the Word of God

transformed them. They refused to be conformed, but they were transformed in their mind about God. They were sold out and their mind was made up. They had the same mind be in them, that is also in Christ Jesus. I imagine they regurgitated scriptures as,

Fear thou not; for I am with thee: be not dismayed; for I am thy God: I will strengthen thee; yea, I will help thee; yea, I will uphold thee with the right hand of my righteousness. (Isaiah 41:10) KJV

When thou walkest through the fire, thou shalt not be burned; neither shall the flame kindle upon thee. (Isaiah 43:2) KJV

The young men knew what the Word said, regarding idols. They knew what the king did was wicked and unacceptable. Their reality was that, they never needed to decide nor make a choice. They served God and not Baal.

9Therefore God also has highly exalted Him and given Him the name which is above every name, 10that at the name of Jesus every knee should bow, of those in heaven, and of those on earth and of those under the earth 11and that every tongue should confess that Jesus Christ is Lord, to the glory of God the Father.
(Philippians 2:9-11) KJV

God elevated Jesus to a place of the highest honor. His name is above any name that is named. His name has the authority that, at His name, every knee will bow. It can be a knee in heaven, on earth, and under earth; all will bow. They will also use their tongue to speak and confess that Jesus is Lord of all. Everyone will recognize Jesus' authority. They will recognize His right to be king of Kings and LORD of Lords.

19Then was Nebuchadnezzar full of fury (which mean there was no room within him for anything else), he form of his visage (look, appearance, expression, countenance) was changed against Shadrach, Meshach and Abednego: therefore he spake. 20and commanded that they should heat the furnace one seven times (God's number of completion) more than it was wont to be heated. And he commanded the most mighty men that were in his army to bind Shadrach, Meshach and Abednego and to cast them into the burning fiery furnace.

21Then these men were bound in their coats, their hosen and their hats and their other garments and were cast into the midst of the burning fiery furnace. 22Therefore, because the king's commandment was urgent & the furnace exceeding hot, the flames of the fire slew those men that took up Shadrach, Meshach and Abednego. 23And these three men, Shadrach, Meshach and Abednego, fell down bound into the midst of the burning fiery furnace. (Daniel 3:19-23) KJV

The character of the king was self-willed, rigid and cruel. He was easily led away by what others said. He was full of anger that overflowed from earlier anger. He refused to stomach resistance and defiance. His authority was challenged, and this disturbed him. Even his skin had changed colors. The red blood cells rushed to the surface of his face. The facial expression became distorted. Muscles in his body became tensed. His rationale was obscured into a pit of rage. The demonic force, manifested outwardly into a mad man. He was so angry that he demanded fire for the furnace be heated seven times, *(God's number),* hotter than normal. This uncontrolled anger dispatched a spirit of violence and murder. The fire caused the death of his Special Forces soldiers. It consumed them, while they escorted God's three men to the furnace. His desire for their death caused him to really shoot himself, when his men died.

The furnace was hot, but the king was even hotter. He was determined the defiant men should not escape the unprescribed or uncontrolled fire. I imagined, the king knew he would have a cremation service for them. They were thrown into the furnace fully clothed. If their clothes remained, it would be more excruciating. Clothes would stick to the body and make the pain unbearable. All the activities were orchestrated by demonic powers; yet the three young men were *transformers.* They had faith in God. Therefore, they did not fight to prevent entrance into the fire. God is their Source. The unprescribed fire, will now become controlled by their Source.

Then Nebuchadnezzar the king was astonished and rose up in haste, and spake and said unto his counselors, Did not we cast three men bound into the midst of the fire? They answered and said unto the king, True, O king. He answered and said, Lo, I see four men loose, walking in the midst of the fire, and they have no hurt; and the form of the fourth is like the Son of God.

(Daniel 3:24-25) KJV

The unprescribed fire of man became a controlled fire by God

The fire became the manifested controlled fire of God. It was heated seven times because seven is God's number. This should remind us that God was there in the beginning. He was there when the furnace was first heated seven times hotter. The king need not say, the fourth man was the Son of God. No one else could do that, but the Son of God. The young men knew who He was. The three young men did hear a sound, but the sound was not the sound a natural man would hear. It was a Supernatural Spiritual Sound. They prophetically heard the sound of the Coming of the LORD.

For the Lord Himself shall descend from heaven with a shout, with the voice of the archangel and with the trump (through ministers of God also) of God and the dead in Christ shall rise first.
(I Thessalonians 4:16) KJV

Jesus, the Son of God Himself, literally came through the sky with a shout to rescue them in their worst trial. He came to *rapture* them out of their trial, tribulation, circumstance or situation. The dead in Christ shall rise. The dead in Christ are those that remain focused on God. The dead in Christ are those that have denied themselves during the fires. They were dead to themselves and their desires. The dead in Christ will rise out of the fire. The dead in Christ are those that cannot see naturally but sees spiritually. The dead in Christ are those that cannot feel anything naturally. The dead in Christ are those that have been changed from corruptible seed to incorruptible seed. The dead in Christ have risen out of doctrine of men, tradition and religion. The Coming of the Lord does not surprise the dead in Christ. They know there is always a Coming of the Lord to *rapture* them out. He Comes as a doctor, mind regulator, deliverer, way-maker, lawyer and sustainer. He Comes in the midst of a motor vehicle accident, financial advisor, burden-bearer etc.

God is in the midst of the fire of *transformers*. All that call upon the Name of Jesus, shall be saved at the Coming of the Lord.

Jesus turns the unprescribed/uncontrolled fire Into a controlled fire

He makes what man meant for evil and turns it around for good. He causes all things to work together for good, for those that love God and is called according to His purpose. Uncontrolled fires started by others in an attempt, to get rid of us, become controlled fires. God is there to control them. He comes with a shout and takes over. He never leaves nor forsake us. He is the fourth man; the Son of Man in the fire. He is with us always, even until the end of the world, even in the fire.

The fire God controls becomes a refiner's fire. In a controlled fire, He removes debris from our lives. He baptizes us with the Holy Ghost and with Fire in this controlled fire. He teaches us to trust and have faith in Him, in the process of this controlled fire. He ensures when we walk through fire we will not be burned in this controlled fire. He reassures us that when we submit to Him, resist the devil, Satan flees, in this controlled fire. He gives us the peace of God that surpasses all understanding that will keep our heart and mind in Christ Jesus in this controlled fire. He makes us written epistle read and seen of men in this controlled fire. He waits for us to say, "not my will but thou will be done in my life", in this controlled fire. He sees to it that our praises go up so blessings can come down in this controlled fire.

The king saw something that sparked fear within him. The three young men were not down, bound or hurt. They were walking around in the furnace. They had just experienced the Coming of the Lord. I imagine they were walking around praising God, who had come quickly to save them. God had delivered them not from the furnace, but while in the furnace.

26Then Nebuchadnezzar came near to the mouth of the burning fiery furnace, and spake, and said, Shadrach, Meshach, and Abednego, ye servants of the most high God, come forth, and come hither. Then Shadrach, Meshach and Abednego, came forth of the midst of the fire. 27And the princes, governors, and captains, and the king's counsellors, being gathered together, saw these men, upon whose bodies the fire had no power, nor was an hair of their head singed, neither were their coats changed, nor the smell of fire had passed on them. (Daniel 3:26-27) KJV

The king had summoned the deadliest force of nature with his tongue. His words spoken out of his mouth started this fire. James says, "A fire set by the tongue and its words can set a forest (people) on fire." In this case God controlled the fire, which the tongue tried to set. The fire upon the king's tongue did not obey the king, but that fire obeyed God's tongue. Touch not my anointed. The king ordered the three men out of the furnace and recognized their God. This time the three young men obeyed the king and emerged from the furnace. This is perfect deliverance from a death by fire experience. This deliverance manifested supernaturally from heaven at the Coming of the Lord. Scripture said, the fire had no power. The fire had no power because this is an unprescribed fire that God took and made it a controlled fire.

IN THE CONTROLLED FIRE
A NATURAL FIRE HAS NO POWER

The fire helped the men of God, instead of harming them. It consumed their bonds or bondage and gave them liberty. Whom the SON make free is free indeed! It launched them into a new level in God. It gave them more power and authority. When caught in a controlled fire, others gleefully gather to witness our demise. They gathered to see if we are burning. They gathered to see the fire did not burn our hair. They gathered to see the fire did not burn our clothes. They gathered and sensed our clothes did not smell like smoke. They gathered and saw we did not die. All this occurred because we stayed focused on God in an uncontrolled fire.

28Then Nechadnezzar spake and said, Blessed be the God of Shadrach, Meshach and Abednego who hath sent His angel & delivered his servants that trusted in him and have changed the king's word and have yielded their bodies that they might not serve nor worship any god, except their own God. 29Therefore, I make a decree, That every people, nation and language, which speak anything amiss against the God of Shadrach, Meshach, and Abednego, shall be cut in pieces (limb from limb), and their houses shall be made a dunghill: because there is no other God that can deliver after this sort. 30Then the king promoted Shadrach, Meshach, and Abednego, in the province of Babylon.
Daniel 3: 28-30) KJV

In the Coming of the Lord, God rescued His servants because they had faith in Him. They refused to allow outside influences of fear and death to deter their faith. They refuse to violate the first commandment. They refused to give up. They believed God with all their heart, mind, soul and body. They did not look at what was happening on the outside. They remained focused. In other words, they kept their eyes and mind on Jesus. He kept them in perfect peace. The king credited their deliverance in the unprescribed fire to their faith in God.

WHY ALL THE MIRACLES OCCURRED

It was because they ignored all the threats of the king. They ignored the orders of death. They also laid their lives on the line, rather than worship a gold image. After that, a new decree went into effect. It stated that anyone, anywhere, of any race, creed or color, who spoke against the God of Shadrach, Meshach and Abednego will be cut into pieces, limb by limb. Homes would be demolished. It became illegal to speak against their God. The king had never seen a God pull off a rescue like the one he saw. Their God is the greatest. Shadrach, Meshach, and Abednego were promoted because of their faith in God. Promotion came because an uncontrolled/unprescribed fire did not spook them. They knew God controlled all fires. They refused to compromise. They refused to manipulate their way out of the fire. They remained until God had come Himself to rescue them. When we are placed in unprescribed fires, God takes over and makes it a controlled fire. In the end, the king was humbled and transformed by the *transformers* that were in an unprescribed fire.

FIRE IS GOOD FOR PEOPLE AND LAND

After years of fire prevention, it was discovered that an environment (Christian) without periodic fires becomes unhealthy. Controlled, prescribed fires and burning is known as hazard (danger) reduction. It is used in forest management, farming and grass restoration (people are known as trees and need restoration as well as renewal). Trees are stressed by overcrowding. Men as trees must be pruned with the tools of God for unwanted flesh (too many excess appendages, not of God). After prescribed fire burns excess debris; new growth is promoted. The right fire at the right place, at the right time, reduces hazardous fuels, recycles nutrients into the forest; protects communities from extreme fires; decrease spread of pest and disease; removes unwanted species threats to the environment; provides food for animals; improves habitat for endangered species; recycles nutrients back into soil; promotes trees and plant growth.

When God prescribe the right fire at the right place for the right time or specific situations in our lives, it reduces:
(1) Hazardous fuel or odors that are not sweet-smelling savor to God's nostrils
(2) Recycles members into the church through The Great Commission
(3) Protects the community of God from extreme strange fires
(4) Minimizes the spread of pests and disease among the sheep
(5) Removes the unwanted species that threaten the church as cliques, divisions and form of godliness and denying the power there of
(6) Provide spiritual food for the members
(7) Improves the spiritual habitat for the lamb and the sheep

(8) Promotes the spiritual growth in the sheep

(9) Promotes the use of the spiritual gifts in decency and order

More prescribed fires of God mean fewer extreme wildfires in the church. Just as burn plans are prescribed. God also write burn plans and prescribed fires for the believers. He identifies the best conditions in which believers will burn safely for the best results. Burn plans identify or prescribe the best conditions, under which trees and other plants will burn, to get the best results safely.

A burn plan stimulates growth and renewal in the natural forest and in the believers. Germination is the process by which a plant grows from a seed. We are to germinate or die (to our will) to grow from the seed of the Word. Germination is the seed (us) expanding into a greater tree from a small seed. Germination depends on both internal (heart) and external (lifestyle) conditions. The external factors as the right temperature (hot, cold, lukewarm), water (washing of water of word), oxygen (Holy Spirit lead and guide) and light or darkness (kingdom of God or kingdom of Satan) are important. All plants need these (cooperate anointing, prayer, praise, worship, read word, teaching, church attendance) to be successful seed germination. According to the individual seed and its connection, it will either dwarf or grow.

Here is an example of a prescribed fire, controlled by God for His man of God

Prescribe means to set, agreed, given, prearranged, approved, recommended and advised. These were Paul's many trials or fires he went through to know God.

16Again I say, don't think that I am a fool to talk like this. But even if you do, listen to me, as you would to a foolish person, while I also boast a little. 17Such boasting is not from the Lord, but I am acting like a fool. 18And since others boast about their human achievements, I will, too. 19After all, you think you are so wise, but you enjoy putting up with fools! 20You put up with it when someone enslaves you, takes everything you have, takes advantage of you, takes control of everything, and slaps you in the face.

21I'm ashamed to say that we've been too "weak" to do that! But whatever they dare to boast about—I'm talking like a fool again I dare to boast about it, too. 22Are they Hebrews? So am I. Are they Israelites? So am I. Are they descendants of Abraham? So am I. 23Are they servants of Christ? I know I sound like a madman, but I have served him far more. I have worked harder, been put in prison more often, been whipped times without number, and faced death again and again.

24Five different times the Jewish leaders gave me thirty-nine lashes. 25Three times I was beaten with rods. Once I was stoned. Three times I was shipwrecked. Once I spent a whole night and a day adrift at sea. 26I have traveled on many long journeys. I have faced danger from rivers and from robbers. I have faced danger from my own people, the Jews, as well as from the Gentiles. I have faced danger in the cities, in the deserts, and on the seas. And I have faced danger from men who claim to be believers but are not. 27I have worked hard and long, enduring many sleepless nights. I have been hungry and thirsty and have often gone without food. I have shivered in the cold, without enough clothing to keep me warm.

28Then, besides all this, I have the daily burden of my concern for all the churches. 29Who is weak without my feeling that weakness? Who is led astray, and I do not burn with anger? 30If I must boast, I would rather boast about the things that show how weak I am. 31God, the Father of our Lord Jesus, who is worthy of eternal praise, knows I am not lying. 32When I was in Damascus, the governor under King Aretas kept guards at the city gates to catch me. 33I had to be lowered in a basket through a window in the city wall to escape from him.
(II Corinthians 11:16-33 NLT)

5And you have forgotten the exhortation which speaks to you as to sons: "My son, do not despise the chastening of the LORD, *Nor be discouraged when you are rebuked by Him; 6For whom the* LORD *loves He chastens, And scourges every son whom He receives."*

7You endure chastening, God deals with you as with sons; for what son is there whom a father does not chasten? 8But if you are without chastening, of which all have become partakers, then you are illegitimate and not sons. 9Furthermore, we have had human fathers who corrected us, and we paid them respect. Shall we not much more readily be in subjection to the Father of spirits and live? 10 For they indeed for a few days chastened us as seemed best to them, but He for our profit, that we may be partakers of His holiness. 11Now no chastening seems to be joyful for the present, but painful; nevertheless, afterward it yields the peaceable fruit of righteousness to those who have been trained by it.

12Therefore strengthen the hands which hang down, and the feeble knees, 13 and make straight paths for your feet, so that what is lame may not be dislocated, but rather be healed.

14Pursue peace with all people, and holiness, without which no one will see the Lord: (Hebrews 12: 5:14 NKJV)

Ultimately, when we are tested in fire, some of us will conform, some of us will inform, and some of us will transform. Unprescribe means not set, not agreed upon, not given, not prearranged, not approved, not recommended and not advised. Prescribes means set, agreed, given, prearranged, approved, recommended and advised. Uncontrolled means out of controlled, not regulated, out of order, deviation from the original, undisciplined, non-compliant, and not submissive. Controlled means govern, guide, regulate, compliant, discipline or submitted.

If a person is taking blood pressure medications and their blood pressure increases or is out of control, it may be due to non-compliant, to a diet, exercise and medications. They have caused this effect.

There are fires in many of our lives out of controlled, due to sparks we caused, others caused, and God allowed them to remain. God allowed these fires to continue, because it gives Him opportunity to control uncontrolled fires.

THE FIRE

1 Peter 1:6–7 NABRE, "Now for a little while you may have to suffer various trials, so that the genuineness of your faith, more precious than gold, which though perishable is tested by fire, may rebound (prove to be genuine) to praise and glory & honor at the revelation of Jesus Christ."

Peter wrote to the Christians that were suffering persecution because of their testimony for Christ. He reminds them that they could have joy in sorrow. They could also have joy in the knowledge that various trials were only for a season or a little while; whereas the glory will be forever. Their suffering is for a purpose and they in turn will bear much fruit.

11th APPROACH

When There Is No King In the Land

In those days there was no king in Israel; everyone did what was right in his own eyes.   (Judges 21:25) KJV

Whenever a King speaks, His words are backed with power. That word from the King's mouth has the capability within that word, to bring life to any death situation. His words are absolute and not subject to challenge by others. In Judges 19, we will explore events that occurred when Israel did not have a king in the land or their life. This is a vivid picture of how lives can be in disarray without a King; disorder is inevitable.

Ecclesiastes 8:4 AKJV says, "Where the word of a King is, there is power: and who may say unto Him, what doest thou?"

EVERY MAN DID THAT WHICH WAS RIGHT IN HIS OWN EYES

God desires to establish His Kingdom, influence and authority in the land and in our lives. This can only be done through man's obedience and conformity to the voice of our King; Jesus. Therefore, the knowledge of the glory of the King's kingdom will have opportunity to manifest throughout the earth, as the gospel is preached. The earth will be filled with His glory as water cover the sea.

For the earth shall be filled with the knowledge of the glory of the Lord, as the water covers the sea.   (Habakkuk 2:14) KJV

    The glory will cover the earth, when the king is in our body, land and becomes a lifestyle. Barnes Notes on the bible states; "For the Spirit of the Lord filled the earth and when He filled it, the earth was filled with the knowledge of the glory of the Lord, so that unlearned and ignorant men became wise and eloquent, and earthly became heavenly, yea, they who were earthly became heaven, knowing the glory of the Lord, declaring the glory of God, as waters cover the sea."
    The knowledge of the glory of God covers the earth, when the King's heavenly legislation rule in our land, lives and lifestyle. God allowed the children of Israel to journey forty years through the wilderness to learn who and what ruled their hearts. Their hearts went through a continuous cycle of rebellion against God. They refused to allow the King, God's authority and influence rule them.
    When there is no King in the land or our lives, the voice of the Father is absent. Therefore, depravity has

opportunity to join itself to our lives. If there is a little leaven from outside influence, it could take over. When there is no King in the land, a little leaven, leavens the whole loaf. In Galatians 5:9, the loaf designed to empower people to rise for Christ, instead rise for the kingdom of darkness.

Galatians 5:7-10 NIV says, *7You were running a good race. Who cut in on you to keep you from obeying the truth? 8That kind of persuasion does not come from the one who calls you. 9A little yeast works through the whole batch of dough. 10 I am confident in the Lord that you will take no other view. The one who is throwing you into confusion, whoever that may be, will have to pay the penalty.*

There must be a ruler. When there is no king in the land, someone will give directives. As we learn in this chapter, man becomes his own influential directive voice. At times, right is call wrong and wrong is call right. At times, there is a form of godliness that denies the power thereof. Time can entangle. For the time is coming when society won't listen to sound doctrine as stated in the Message Bible,

3You're going to find that there will be times when people will have no stomach for solid teaching but will fill up on spiritual junk food—catchy opinions that tickle their fancy. 4They'll turn their backs on truth and chase mirages. (II Timothy 4:3-4) MSG

God intend for man to rule by His authority, influence and voice. When there is no King in the land, the voice of the King is not heard. Though we have ears to hear, we do not hear. Another voice has the ability to magnify natural things beyond spiritual things. Satan's strategies, rules and regulations make natural things seem more important than spiritual things. Other voices can parade as an angel of light. They may look, sound and appear to do and be like God. Be aware that Satan is the father of lies. Wherever the kingdom of God is found, the King is the head, the ruler, the influence and the voice in the land or in a person's life. When the King rule and reign, the people become Full of Consistent and Unlimited Sight into the things of God. We will examine different people in Judges 19; without the King in their land or life and they were *unfocused*.

These scriptures reveal the Israelites, the concubine and a Levite without the King in neither their land nor lives

1And it came to pass in those days, when there was no king in Israel, that there was a certain Levite sojourning on the side of mount Ephraim, who took to him a concubine out of Bethlehem Judah. 2And his concubine played the whore against him, and went away from him unto her father's house to Bethlehem Judah, and was there four whole months. 3And her husband arose, and went after her, to speak friendly unto her, and to bring her again, having his servant with him, and a couple of asses: and she brought him into her father's house: and when the father of the damsel saw him, he rejoiced to meet him. (Judges 19: 1-3) KJV

There was no King in the land of the Israelites, the Levite nor the concubine. Israel was independent from God. They orchestrated laws according to their own standards, benefitting themselves. Leaving God out of their lives reduced them to undertaking any and everything. There was no discipline, authority, head, king, voice, ruler, influence, regulations or rules to lead and guide them. Everyone did what they thought were right and pleasurable in their own eyesight. They were governed by their own accord. Without God they had no spiritual head or covering. For example, there was a concubine from Bethlehem Judah. She is symbolic of one that had previously served God with all her heart, mind, soul and body. When Jesus is accepted as Savior, a person becomes married to Him. They became the Bride and He their Bridegroom. Ephesians 5:25-27, speaks on this.

25Husbands, love your wife as Christ also loved the church and gave Himself up for her, 26So that He might sanctify her, having cleansed her by the washing of water with the word, that He might present to Himself the church in all her glory, having no spot or wrinkle or any such thing; but that she would be holy and blameless. Let us rejoice and exalt and give Him the glory, for the marriage of the Lamb has come, 27and His Bride has made herself ready; it was granted her to clothe herself with fine linen, bright bright and pure, for the fine linen is the righteous deed of the saints.   *(Ephesians 25-27 KJV)*

7Let us rejoice and be glad and give him glory! For the wedding of

the Lamb has come, and his bride has made herself ready. 8Fine linen, bright and clean, was given her to wear. 9And the angel said to me, "write this; Blessed are those who are invited to the marriage supper of the Lamb". These are the true words of God.
(Revelation 19:7-9) NIV

    The concubine from Bethlehem Judah married a man of God. This man of God, a Levite, was not a good example as a leader. His marriage was approved by the law, but not by God. Once married, it became a covenant. Covenants are important to God. During bible days, having a concubine as a wife was accepted in Israel. She was considered a lower-class wife. Her primary duties included performing sexual pleasures, bearing children and making contributions in running the household. Ultimately, she had no privileges nor received inheritances as a legal wife. According to spiritual laws, when a concubine left her husband, she backslides. We see the concubine leaves her husband. This is spiritually symbolic of what the scriptures calls backslider. Jeremiah 3:14 speak of God calling Israel backsliding children in. It says, "Turn, O backsliding children," saith the Lord; "For I am married unto you: and I will take you one of a city and two of a family, and I will bring you to Zion."

    The concubine gave way for the absenteeism of the voice of God. She left her spouse. This gave her the freedom to do what is right in her own sight. She is independent of God. There is no king, authority, voice or directives in her life. Any leaven from outside influences could take over. Remember, Satan is the enemy to God. Without the ear to hear the Holy Spirit guidance, it could cause lawlessness entrance. Without the King in her land, sound counsel was void.

There could be many reasons why the woman, church or backslider may have left home. If we look her in the eye of being a wife to a man of God, or Levite in the church, the picture may become clearer. Maybe people considered her inferior and treated her as such. Could they have whispered about her since she was a concubine? Had she been a street woman that tried to clean her life up? Was she secondary to everyone else? Was she placed on the shelf until later? Being a previous whore, was her sin life really covered by the members with their love? Was she privileged to the elite circle, cliques, or gatherings? Could it be that, she was a body part in church, and felt she just did not fit? She was legally attached and presumes to be fitly joined, together with the body. She had received Jesus and became a part of the family of God one Sunday morning. Maybe none of the above reasons caused her to leave. Could it be, she just had an issue?

She had a genuine calling into the ministry. She was called to the reproductive organs of ministry. It is similar to the function of reproductive organs in the natural body. Her purpose is to reproduce sons of God to look just like Jesus. She produced well in the church, by the fruit of her womb. Yet unnoticed! She reads the vision of the house and run with the production of it. Though married, maybe she did not feel loved. It appears in the natural, she is loved, but in her heart, she is an outcast. Therefore, she decides to submit to another voice and leaves. She believed the voice that told her to leave. The voice sounds like Jesus. The voice seems to be godly. The voice seems to lead and guides like the Holy Spirit. Since there was no King in her land any more, she decides to do as she pleased. She had ears to hear but stop hearing. She had a heart to understand but stop understanding. She had eyes to see but stop seeing. Therefore, the scripture about husband and wife being one is foreign. Therefore, the other voice instructs her to leave.

Her life as a concubine made it easy to fall back into old habits. Therefore, she pursued other lovers. Other lovers dictated the type authority she desired to rule her life. Thou shall have no other gods, or lovers before Me, is what God says. She left God to follow voices whispering lies into her ear. As scripture stated, she played the whore or harlot against her spouse. This means she deserted him. She moved into immorality. There was no provision for a woman that divorced a man, but she left anyway. She broke covenant with the King, for the lovers of deception, lies, the world, sexual pleasure, fleshy desires, anger, backsliding, rejection, thirst and anything that made her drunk with wine. She became full of and drunk on the things of the flesh. She certainly was not drunk on Holy Spirit.

Many considered the concubine's husband as a decent man. He appeared as though he really loved her. After four months had passed, he decided to go and persuade her to return home. The husband is seen as trying to reconcile with her. After all, he did leave the ninety-nine to go after her. He showed the character, qualities and integrity of a good husband and man of God. When he found her, she was at her father's house. He seemed relieved and happy to see her because he was pleasant to her. He acted as though he had forgiven her for leaving.

Notice how the concubine returned to a place she once was familiar with. She knew she would be received there. She would not feel an inferiority complex or as an outcast. She went to a place where the authority had once spoken into her life. She went to this place because she really did long for a King in her land. She needed the rules, regulations, discipline, authority, direction and voice of a Father. She needed to be appreciated and loved. The concubine went to her Father's house. In her father's house are many mansions (dwelling places, temples).

I imagined she needed to be one of the mansions, or dwelling places for Holy Spirit. She had been around those that were said to be mansions. Except, she wonders what spirit did they house? There was no King in their land or the system where the Levite had been churched. They were temples that displayed a way that seem right to man, but the end would be destruction. The concubine wanted to be a part of something with spiritual life, not a part of the system.

ANOTHER EXAMPLE OF NO KING IN THE LAND OF THE LEVITE NOR HIS FATHER-IN-LAW

4And his father in law, the damsel's father, retained him; and he abode with him three days: so they did eat and drink, and lodged there. 5And it came to pass on the fourth day, when they arose early in the morning, that he rose up to depart: and the damsel's father said unto his son in law, Comfort thine heart with a morsel of bread, and afterward go your way. 6And they sat down, and did eat and drink both of them together: for the damsel's father had said unto the man, Be content, I pray thee, and tarry all night, and let thine heart be merry. 7And when the man rose up to depart, his father in law urged him: therefore he lodged there again.

8And he arose early in the morning on the fifth day to depart; and the damsel's father said, Comfort thine heart, I pray thee. And they tarried until afternoon, and they did eat both of them. 9And when the man rose up to depart, he, and his concubine, and his servant, his father in law, the damsel's father, said unto him, Behold, now the day draweth toward evening, I pray you tarry all night: behold, the day groweth to an end, lodge here, that thine heart may be merry; and tomorrow get you early on your way, that thou mayest go home. 10 But the man would not tarry that night, but he rose up and departed, and came over against Jebus, which is Jerusalem; and there were with him two asses saddled, his concubine also was with him.   *(Judges 19:4-10) KJV*

  When the Levite or man of God went to fetch the concubine, afterward, he planned to visit the temple of

God. But upon his arrival to his father-in- law's place, he stayed longer than anticipated. This was an indication that there was no King in his land; the voice of authority did not tell him he had to leave. Though he was a man of God, he was part of a system that did not lead nor guide him into all truth. He was moved by the voice of his carnal nature. He had no discipline to move and go to the temple of God. He submitted to kindness and persuasion of man, which had no King, authority and direction in his land either.

The Levite, man of God became a pleaser of men. The host with his hospitality, kindness and persuasion, prevented the Levite from doing the Father's business. His heart was not really geared toward going to the temple of God. A man with the heart of God would go about doing his father's business. This temporary pleasure prevented him from doing the work of the Lord. He became slothful taking pleasure in staying away from the temple of God. The father in law detained him for five days eating, drinking and becoming merry. The man of God became idle, and lived as a person that had no King, direction, voice, guidance or authority in his land.

There was no king or voice of authority in this leader's life; therefore, he could not discern the traps of Satan. He could not discern the deception of Satan in detaining him. Luke 16:8 says, "The children of the world are wiser than the children of light." Hospitality blinded the vision of the man of God from his purpose.

The father in-law was more concerned about his reputation, than his son in law getting to the temple of God. Each time the Levite tried to leave with his concubine, her father urged him to rest a little longer. Each day was a carbon copy of the day before. The man of God did not recognize the schemes, strategies and methodologies of Satan. Satan will use people, places and things to manipulate. This is how he ensured that the voice of the King never enter in the Levites land.

The father in law's abundance of hospitality appeared to be the right thing to do. It was a set up to prevent the man of God from carrying out the Father's business. The religious leader did not discern the devices of Satan because there was no King, nor voice of the Holy Spirit to guide him. Finally, the Levite was determined to leave. He left on the evening of day number five. His servant saddled the two donkeys, so he and his concubine could leave. They headed in the way toward Jebus or Jerusalem, which was six miles from Bethlehem.

Example of no king in the land of the Levite nor the people of Gibeah

11 And when they were by Jebus, the day was far spent; and the servant said unto his master, Come, I pray thee, and let us turn in into this city of the Jebusites, and lodge in it. 12 And his master said unto him, We will not turn aside hither into the city of a stranger, that is not of the children of Israel; we will pass over to Gibeah. 13 And he said unto his servant, Come, and let us draw near to one of these places to lodge all night, in Gibeah, or in Ramah. 14 And

> *they passed on and went their way; and the sun went down upon them when they were by Gibeah, which belongeth to Benjamin. 15 And they turned aside thither, to go in and to lodge in Gibeah: and when he went in, he sat him down in a street of the city: for there was no man that took them into his house to lodging.*
>
> *(Judges 19: 11-15) KJV*

It was very late in the evening and growing dark, when the servant suggested they find shelter in the Jebusite town. The Levite refused to listen to his servant. He said they could not stay in a town, where there were no Israelites. He was reluctant to receive hospitality from non-Israelites. They went further on to Gibeah or Ramah. The man of God was forced to stay in Gibeah, a town in the land of Benjamin. He did not want to go to the city of the Jebusites. They hoped someone would see them and give them lodging, but no one obliged them. They sat in darkness in the street. There was no voice of authority nor King in the Levite's land. Therefore, he submitted to his own will and voice.

He refused not to associate with non-Israelites. He was adamant about living in corruption. The people were known as outcasts. He would not be seen near them. The Levite only wanted to associate with those he felt was as godly as he. His behavior revealed the prejudices within his heart. He considered himself a man of status. He refused to associate with anyone, except those of his status.

There was no voice of the King in his land. He dare not associate with the oppressed, hungry, blind, naked poor, Gentiles or common people. His servant tried advising him otherwise, but he would not listen. He did not receive the word of wisdom about things that were to come. If he had the King in his land, he would have recognized the Holy Spirit's voice in his servant. The voice of the King would have told him not to walk in the darkness. Now he will be like a blind man walking in darkness, oblivious of the direction and path he is headed.

Therefore, the man of God sat in the street with his servant and concubine. None of the inhabitants of Gibeah wanted to associate with him. Yet, he wanted to associate with them. He was a stranger in his own people's land. He wanted to lodge with the people of Gibeah's religious system had no King, authority, head, rules, regulation or voice in their land. The man felt he was a man of status, yet no one paid attention to Him. The people hearts were hard hearted, lawless with degraded character. What the Levite didn't know was that he would have been better off in the land of those he despised, than in Gibeah.

EXAMPLE OF A MAN THAT STARTED OUT WITH THE KING IN HIS LAND, FOCUSED BUT BECAME UNFOCUSED

16And, behold, there came an old man from his work out of the field at even, which was also of mount Ephraim; and he sojourned in Gibeah: but the men of the place were Benjamites. 17And when he had lifted up his eyes, he saw a wayfaring man in the street of the city: and the old man said, Whither goest thou? and whence comest thou? 18And he said unto him, We are passing from Bethlehem Judah toward the side of mount Ephraim; from thence am I: and I went to Bethlehem-judah, but I am now going to the house of the Lord; and there is no man that receiveth me to house.

19Yet there is both straw and provender for our asses; and there is bread and wine also for me, and for thy handmaid, and for the young man which is with thy servants: there is no want of any thing. 20And the old man said, Peace be with thee; howsoever let all thy wants lie upon me; only lodge not in the street. 21So he brought him into his house, and gave provender unto the asses: and they washed their feet, and did eat and drink.
(Judges 19:16-21) KJV

There arrived an old man from the same neck of the woods as the Levite. He was an Ephraimite. He showed his hospitality and compassion toward them. The old man decided to provide lodging for the Levite, his wife and servant. He was relieved, the Levite accepted the offer.

The Benjamites, which are the inhabitants of this city of Gibeah, did not take in the Levite. They passed by him without any offer to assist him. These were the same people the Levite wanted to be with when he passed by the town of Jebus. These were people whom he believed to be his people; the ones with status. They are a part of this religious system. If anyone should help a stranger, it should be the Benjamites of Gibeah. They should be familiar with a stranger, being in the street and appreciate giving him a helping hand. After all, their ancestor Benjamin was born on the road as his mother traveled. If any should be kind to anyone, it is they. These religious people with status forgot where God brought them.

The story of the Good Samaritan in Luke 10 is like this event. A traveler was stripped of his clothes and beaten very badly. He was left on the road alone to possibly die, just as the Levite, the woman and his servant were left. The religious leaders' system of the priest and a Levite saw the wounded man on the road. They did nothing to assist him, as the Benjamites did nothing to assist the Levite. A common man called a Good Samaritan found the wounded man. He took care of him, even though the culture, at that time, was Samaritans and Jews had no dealings with one another. He ensured the innkeeper continued to nurse the man back to life. He was willing to pay him if additional fees accumulated, during the task of care. The Samaritan promised to settle the debt the next time when he returns. Since there was no King, authority or voice in the land of the religious system of the priest and the Levite, they moved into areas unbecoming for men of God.

Example of no King in the land of the Ephraimite man, the Levite nor the Gibeonites

22Now as they were making their hearts merry, behold, the men of the city, certain sons of Belial, beset the house round about, and beat at the door, and spake to the master of the house, the old man, saying, Bring forth the man that came into thine house, that we may know him. 23 And the man, the master of the house, went out unto them, and said unto them, Nay, my brethren, nay, I pray you, do not so wickedly; seeing that this man is come into mine house, do not this folly. 24 Behold here is my daughter a maiden, and his concubine; them I will bring out now, and humble ye them, and do with them what seemeth good unto you: But unto this man do not so vile a thing. 25 But the men would not hearken to him: so the man took his concubine, and brought her forth unto them; and they knew her, and abused her all the night until the morning: and when the day began to spring, they let her go.

26 Then came the woman in the dawning of the day, and fell down at the door of the man's house where her lord was, till it was light. 27 And her lord rose up in the morning, and opened the doors of the house, and went out to go his way: and, behold, the woman his concubine was fallen down at the door of the house, and her hands were upon the threshold. 28 And he said unto her, up and let us be going. But none answered. Then the man took her up upon an ass, and the man rose up, and gat him unto his place. 29 And when he was come into his house, he took a knife, and laid hold on his concubine, and divided her, together with her bones, into twelve pieces, and sent her into all the coasts of Israel. 30 And it was so, that all that saw it said, there was no such deed done nor seen from the day that the children of Israel came up out of the land of Egypt unto this day: consider of it, take advice, speak your minds.

(Judges 19:22-30) KJV

The host of the home and the Levite were laughing, eating, drinking, rejoicing and being merry. They were having the time of their life. Maybe they had been drinking to the point of drunkenness. They would soon lose their self-control. There was no King, authority, directions or voice in their land. A drunken man sees in his mind, the bold things he could do. Choices made during that time could cause devastation, turn laughter into mourning and joy into sadness.

In this city, men were called the Benjamites. Actually, they were Gibeonites from the Tribe of Benjamin. They had no King, authority, rule, voice, head or discipline in their lives. They were once Christians at one time in their lives, but now are referred to as the sons of Belial. They are children of the devil and are influenced by him. Belial means worthless scoundrels, bent on evil. It is the personification of wickedness, worthlessness and lawlessness. They strongly moved under the influence of lust and abandon the character of God.

The Benjamites offered no hospitality to the Levite, but now they wanted to violate him. They wanted to actively engage in practices that scriptures condemned. They are at the point of reduction to Sodom and Gomorrah. Their acts began when the sons of Belial and the satanic forces of Satan, circled the house so no one could escape. These were a band of sexual perverts that had no King, discipline, rules, direction or authority in their land or life. Forcefully, they pounded fiercely on the door, demanding to get in. They were determined to enter one way or another. Their behavior indicated the door could either be broken down easily or opened for them. They demanded the host bring the Levite out, so they could get to know him. They did not mean that they wanted to learn his name, occupation or how he was doing today. They wanted to know him in an unnatural way. They wanted gratification in the most brutish way. The Law of Moses forbade what they wanted to do.

If a man also lie with mankind, as he lieth with a woman, both of them have committed an abomination: they shall surely be put to death; their blood shall be upon them. (Leviticus 20:13) KJV

These filthy affections dishonored Him. For even their women changed the natural use of their body into that which is against nature. Likewise, the men, leaving the natural use of the woman, burned in their lust one toward another. These men wanted to work that which is unseemingly. And even so they did not like to retain God in their knowledge.

Wherefore, God gave them up to uncleanness through the lust of their own hearts; to dishonor their own bodies between themselves. (Romans 1:24 KJV

These men had no King, voice, discipline, nor authority in their land. God gave them up to disgusting affections. These Benjamites came out of the loins of Jacob; but what happened? There was no King, rule, authority, laws, regulation, head or voice in the land of these religious people. God chosen people had become as wicked as Sodom and Gomorrah.

The host of the home finally opened the door to talk with the men of Gibeah. He pleaded with them not to do this type thing. He tried to appease them by calling them brethren. At one point of time, they had been a land with a King in it. They once practiced being Christians. They could hear the voice of the Holy Spirit, at one time. The Levite as a stranger and guest had come to the Ephramite's house. According to the law of hospitality, he was obligated to protect him. Customs demanded hospitality to be shown to every stranger. It would have been an offense against hospitality and morality if he did not show it. Protecting a guest at any cost ranked at the top of a man's code of honor.

The man of the house began to compromise with the forces of darkness, Satan. He was willing to sacrifice his virgin daughter and the stranger's concubine to wicked men. He suggested they could do with the women, whatever they saw fit to do with them. They could lie with the woman chosen. Do whatever they need to do to satisfy their uncontrolled, violent, burning lust. This man proposed evil, so good could prevail. He had no right to offer the prostitution of his own daughter or the concubine. His act revealed that he was a terrified coward. He saw this as choosing the least of the two evils. Either kill the guest or do unnatural things to his wife. Yet, this religious man allowed, and became a participant in the rape of the woman, church, bride or member. This selfish, carnal man is saving self at the expense of the woman. He did this because he has no King, authority or voice in his land. No King in his land made it easier to sacrifice the woman. He saved self at the expense of another.

The men of Gibeah refused to hear the man of the house, begging them not to do this evil to his guest. They refused to listen but were persistent in wanting the man they lusted for. The men at the door were filled with gross darkness and corrupted flesh. The old man and the Levite both were cowards. This reminds me that the yellow brick road had nothing on the yellow streak that ran down their back.

The Levite finally sent his concubine wife out to the grossly, darkness filled perverts of Gibeah. What happened? He fetched her from her father's house. Now he releases her into a fire of hell. The wicked Benjamites snatched the concubine, as soon as they pulled her in the darkness of evening. She was signed, sealed and delivered to the sons of Belial; the devil. The sons of Belial took the concubine, and they knew her. The religious men of Gibeah assaulted the woman immediately. They joined themselves to her in every unnatural way one could imagine. The concubine, woman, member, whore, bride, wife, harlot and the one with no King in her land, suffered rape at the hands of her attackers. Since the Levite husband was unfocused, and had no King in his land he allowed, participated and consented to the rape of his wife. Maybe now, we see clearly why she left him. This was not a godly choice from a godly man. She was sacrificed to save her hardhearted husband's skin. Both men traded a defenseless woman, to be brutally violated for the entire night until morning.

This woman, whore, person, harlot, church or wife with no KING in her land, suffered the worst possible form of sexual abuse. They assaulted, attacked, abused, misused, battered, beat, mistreated, molested, antagonized, struck, injured, sodomized and whip her all through the night. They used her in the most shocking manner; one after another.

I can imagine the woman drifting off in an unconscious state, just to endure the excruciating, humiliating pain of it all. She probably went into a deep state, hoping, praying, believing and crying out to God. Was she dreaming? Was this a nightmare? She just knew, God would deliver her, but when? God always heard the voice of her tears in the past; but when, this time O LORD? I can hear her thinking; how long Lord God, how long? She brought God into the situation, in her time of crisis, and there will be a coming of the LORD. She will receive Salvation. In her Salvation, she will be protected, made whole, delivered, secured and healed. The Word says, "All that call on the Name of the LORD shall be saved." She visibly saw that, there was a war waging between the kingdom of darkness, and the Kingdom of Light for her soul. Saints were praying, and the devil was playing.

These men of Gibeah had been Christians, children of God. At some point in their lives, they rose out of being ruthless from the world. However, they leaped right back into being ruthless in the world. They could do this because; there was no King, authority or rule in their land or life. Their door was open for evil to enter. The Word of God says a little leaven, leavens the whole loaf. A pinch of sin can corrupt the entire person. They came out into darkness to do evil. In them dwell darkness and there was no Light. Evil will unite many people to become one, just to riot against the kingdom of Light. They became an organize unit of the kingdom of darkness. The demonstration and insurgence of evilness always shows up to kill, steal and destroy.

Sin took the men farther than they intended to go. Sin made them do more than they intended to do. Sin will pay them more wages than they want to be paid. Whenever a woman, wife, member or person is raped by a religious system, the spirit of the sons of Belial is strongest on the scene.

This woman is a prophetic sign detailing the process of Satan's abuse when there is not King, discipline, voice, authority nor the influence of God in our land or life. The woman was released early in the morning. Weeping may endure for a night, but joy comes in the morning. Joy comes because the SON rises in our lives.

The sons of Belial, which is darkness, cannot comprehend the Light. The woman, member, harlot, whore and wife, physically and mentally had to drag her body to the house where everyone in it was out of position. She had to drag herself to a place, where she was supposed to be protected by her husband. She had to drag herself to the same houses that cause her to begin a tempestuous night. She had to drag herself to the place where no one had the King in his land or life.

I can see this woman clearly. The message became the messenger, for it to be delivered as vividly as God reveals it. I imagine, since she had been beaten into a stupor, she was probably in and out of her body. Scripture did say, "To be absent from the flesh is to be present with the LORD." As she had to drag herself to the door of that house, I imagine she had all type visions. She probably saw things to come. She probably saw what the end would be. She probably saw this old man's house as a temporary house of God.

This temporary house of God had an altar. She made it to the bottom of doorway of the house, her altar. It was at the altar where she finally, sacrificed her will for God's will. At the altar she saw herself returning to the church. At the altar she was in a place of protection and refugee. At the altar she was in the place where, she first received the Light. At the altar she was in a place where she would be saved. At the altar she is in a place where she touched the hem of His garment. At the altar she is in a place where she will be made whole.

It was at the altar she fell on her face after a night of torture and humiliation. She used the time on her face to lay prostrate before God. She used this time upon her face as a time to go to God in prayer. She used this time upon her face as a time to wait for God to answer the voice of her tears. She spent time on her face as a time to ask for forgiveness for playing the whore. She used the time on her face as a time to ask forgiveness for backsliding. She used the time on her face as a time to ask forgiveness for those whom abused her. She used the time upon her face as a time to ask forgiveness for her husband whom turned her out.

A threshold is a place that is crossed over to enter another room. Also, a Threshold can take you from one place to another place when you are about to start something new, according to vocabulary com. This woman reached for the Threshold, which is the doorway to get to another room. She reached for the Threshold, which is symbolic of moving from one degree of glory to another degree of glory. She reached for the Threshold, which moves from one side to the *other side*. She reached for the threshold, which is a place where an entirely different state of affairs exists.

Finally, she asked the Father to receive her spirit. Better is her death day than the day she was born. She returned to the dust or dirt she had fallen upon, while suffering abuse the night before. She was finally Home. Old things are passed away, behold all things have become new. She heard this was her new mercy that God gave every morning. This final Threshold was the border she crossed over to go beyond this world, and to another world called Heaven. She reached for the final Threshold that transitioned her from earth to heaven with her Father. He is the King forever in her land.

In the meantime, the religious leader arose the next morning. He had a good night sleep. He opened the door on that morning to leave. He saw the concubine, wife; woman, member, whore and harlot face down. He told her to get up, so they could get going. He was oblivious to her night of horror. He treats her as a piece of property. His insensitivity to her was manifested because he just ordered her to "Get up and let's go!" He could not have possibly phantom what she experienced that previous night. It never entered his mind that she may be injured or even dead. He was cold and did not comprehend how to treat her. There was no compassion for her, even in this broken state.

The woman did not answer him. There was no life in her. She was *dead*. She had given up the Ghost. She was dead due to the excessive abuse in the religious systems of the Benjamites. She was dead because her husband turned her out. She was dead because she was welcomed back from her backslidden state, to go among people with lips. Yet, their heart was far from their words. She was dead because she was naked. She was dead because she was uncovered. She was dead because she was baldheaded. She was dead because there was no King in her land. She was dead because there was no king in the Benjamite's land. Her husband picked her up and placed her on the ass. This is symbolic to the time Jesus told the disciples in Matthew to get an ass for Him.

9Rejoice greatly, O daughter of Zion! Shout in triumph, O daughter of Jerusalem! Behold, your king is coming to you; He is just and endowed with salvation, Humble, and mounted on a donkey, Even on a colt, the foal of a donkey.
(Zachariah 9:9) NASB

This ordeal happened so the scripture can be fulfilled saying, "Say to the daughter of Zion, behold your King is coming to you. We see the coming of the LORD." The King was coming to her, in her land on her death day. Now there is a King in her land and in her life. Again, better is her death day, than the day she was born. This husband did not love her as Christ loved the church. He did not die for her. But, instead she died for him. This woman was a woman of God. She was Christ body. She was Christ church. She was Christ bride. Christ was married to her, the backslider. She was one with Christ. She was bone of His bones. She was flesh of His flesh. What was done to her was done to Christ. What Christ has placed together with Himself, let no man divide asunder.

The husband, Levite and religious leader went home. He was upset and enraged over the treatment of his wife, church, woman, concubine, harlot and whore by the Benjamites. The husband that did not love his wife as Christ loved the church, took her body and divided it into twelve parts with a Sword (Word). There is a body illustration on the following page.

ONE (1) HEAD, ONE (1) NECK, TWO (2) ARMS, TWO (2) HANDS, TWO (2) LEGS, TWO (2) FEET, ONE (1) TORSO, ONE (1) PELVIC

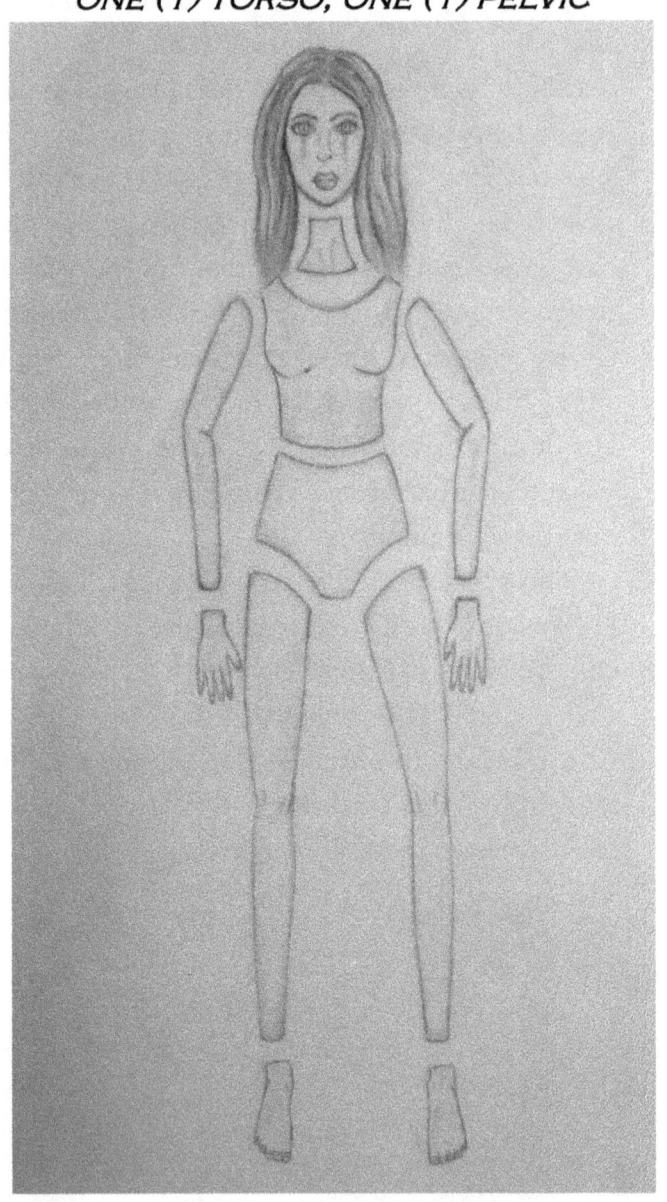

Illustration by Ms. Gabriel Crumpler

He sent a body part to every tribe or church in Israel to send a *Strange Message*. It is a message normally not heard in the pulpit of their tribe or church. The message was about abuse in its most revelatory form. Indignation must be raised about what happened to her He wanted to raise righteous indignation about what the tribe of Benjamin had done to her.

The tribes of Israel or the church saw just what the Levite desired them to see. His mission was accomplished. The men of Gibeah were guilty of this wickedness because there was no King in their land.

For the word of God is quick, and powerful, and sharper than any two-edged sword, piercing even to the dividing asunder of soul and spirit, and of the joints and marrow, and is a discerner of the thoughts and intents of the heart. (Hebrews 4:12 (KJV)

The body parts were infused with the Spirit of God from His Sword. Each time the Levite used His Sword to cut a part off her body, the Word of God, which is the Sword of the Spirit, empowered her body parts with an anointed message to the tribes or church. *This woman was finally moving in her ministry.* Her call and election were sure. Whom God calls, He qualifies. The individual body parts were sent to each church or tribe. The individual parts would prophesy the Word of the LORD. Each body part is a Prophetic Sign with a Prophetic Word. The tribe of Israel and the church saw the divided body of the concubine, bride, church, member, woman, harlot, wife and whore. They heard every word her body parts had to say to the church. She was mangled, abused, raped, tortured, lamed, broken, blinded, hopeless, hurt, powerless and held in captivity at one time. The tribes must physically view and hear the Word of the Lord speaking about this perversion. The Word from Christ's apostle will ask them to, "Consider This. Think on this thing done to Me. My Bride and I are *One*. What you have done to her is done to *Me*. What will you do about this abuse in *My Body*? What is done to His Body is done to Christ." Whatever is done to the least of these is done unto Christ.

I can hear the voice of prophecy to the church, through every one of her body parts. They speak loud and clear. Prophecy or the Word of the LORD came through the one that was stripped of her dignity, character, and livelihood. She was *not* stripped of her destiny. It does not matter what happened to her, she was stilled called. His gifts and calling were without repentance.

ONE HEAD

The head was separated and removed with the sword of the Spirit. It prophesied saying, "My head is a symbol sent to the tribes and churches. My head indicates there was no King in my land nor their land. My head had no voice, rules, regulations, authority nor directions. My head was uncovered, just as their head was uncovered. My head indicates they had battles going on in their mind. All the tribes and churches must have a King in their land. We must have the mind of Christ. Jesus wants a body where He can lay His Head."

One Neck

The neck was separated and removed with the Sword of the Spirit. It prophesied, "My neck is symbolic and indicates the tribes, the church and I, turned away from God. My neck indicates we backslid. It indicated there was no stability in me or them to turn back to God. We must humble ourselves, pray and turn from our wicked ways. We must loose self from the chains around our neck, O captive daughter of Zion."

Two Arms

The two arms were separated and removed with the sword of the Spirit. It prophesied saying, "My arms are symbolic, and indicates no power and strength to resist the wiles of the devil. We must know that the strong right arm of God is raised in victory. God has outstretched arms to help us."

Two Hands

The two hands were separated and removed with the sword of the Spirit. It prophesied, "My hands are symbolic and indicates that my hands, and their hands were put to the plow, and we looked back. My hands and their hands had touched God's anointed. God says to come before Him with pure hands. Our hands are too short to box with God."

Two Legs

The two legs were separated and removed with the sword of the Spirit. It prophesied, "My legs are symbolic and indicates we were weakened in our walk with God. Our legs were useless. God wants them to stand upon their legs, as an exceeding great Army of God."

Two Feet

The two feet were separated and removed with the sword of the Spirit. It prophesied, "My feet and their feet indicate we did not walk on the highway to holiness. We were unclean. But God want us to know, how beautiful are the feet of them that preach the gospel. Their feet are like hind's feet. Their feet are shod with the preparation of the gospel of peace."

One Torso

The one torso was separated and removed with the sword of the Spirit. It prophesied, "My torso is symbolic and indicates that my and their torso had issues in their heart. Those issues flowed out of our mouth. God will create in our torso or chest a clean heart. He will renew a right heart, or the right spirit within our torso. Our torso or chest is covered with the breastplate of righteousness."

ONE PELVIC

The one pelvic was separated and removed with the sword of the Spirit. It prophesied, "My pelvic is symbolic and indicates that my and their pelvic aborted natural and spiritual sons of God from the womb. The sons of Belial had a foothold on us." God said, "His seed is in our pelvic. Greater is He, which is in us, than he that is in the world. He that is in us is of the Holy Ghost. We are the sons of God. There are many sons scheduled to come from our womb or pelvic."

THIS WOMAN WAS THE BODY OF CHRIST

Her body parts spoke the truth and were proof of the terrible act of the Benjamites. The voice of the body spoke loud and clear in the land. The woman that moved away from ministry earlier in her walk with God, now speaks loud and clear from her grave's pulpit. The people will see her body mangled, black, blue, scarred, battered, marked, abused and bruised. They will see the men of Gibeah, the Benjamites, a tribe of Israel perversion toward her.

This rape and assault was as much the Levite's fault, as it was the men of Gibeah's fault. Her husband allowed the rape and murder, which was against the law of God. Whenever there is no king in the land, Satan tempts us to eat fruit God did not ordain. When our focus is diminished, it activates a chain of events in our life. This chain of events has costs. Therefore, receive the body parts prophecy. Hear the Word of the LORD.

> HE THAT HAS AN EAR, LET HIM HEAR
> WHAT THE SPIRIT OF GOD
> IS SAYING UNTO YOU,
> THE CHURCH,
> THE WOMAN AND THE BRIDE…

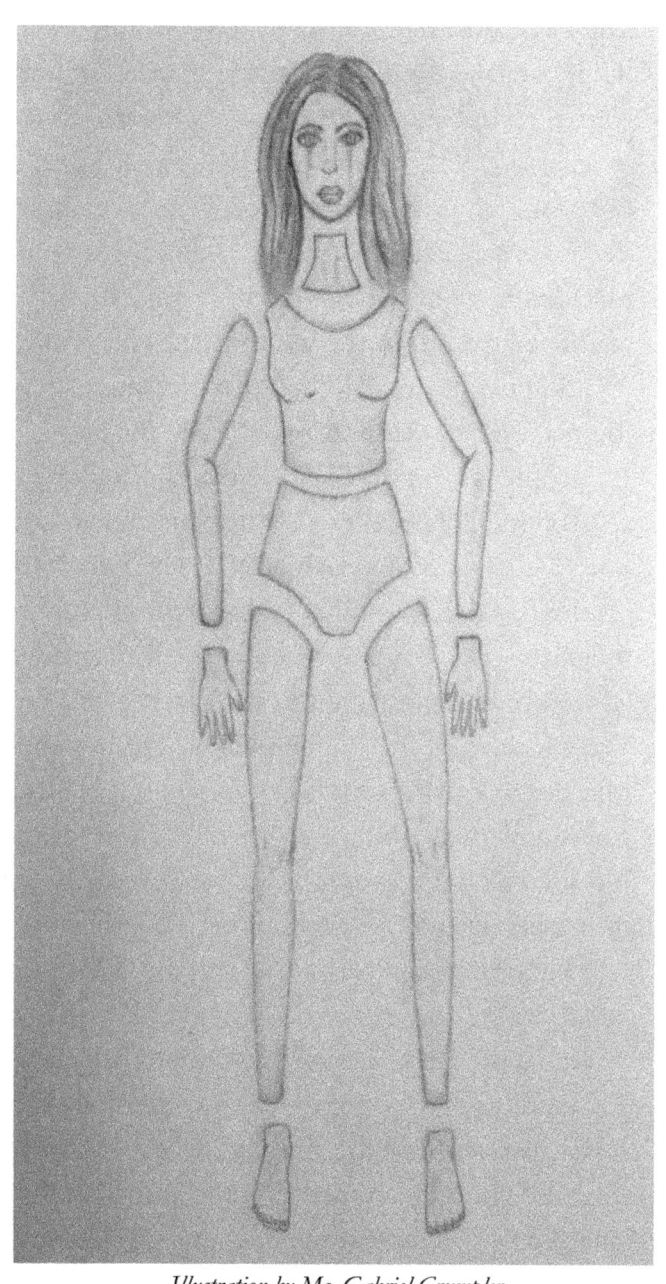

Illustration by Ms. Gabriel Crumpler

In Judges Chapter 20-21, the body parts along with the sword of the Spirit delivered the intended message. Unity among the tribes, Israelites or church members was accomplished. The ones that were outraged needed a response. The nation of Israel was stunned. Chosen warriors from the tribes, except the Benjamites, gathered to hear the Levite tell the story about his wife. The tribes decided to fight the Benjamites, but first they gave them a chance to turn in the guilty parties instead. The tribes would punish them. When the Benjamites refused, war began. The Benjamites had 26,700 men.

In the last battle with the tribes, the Benjamites lost 25,100 men. This almost wiped the Benjaminites Tribe out. There were 600 Benjamite men, which found refuge in the Rock of Rimmon for four months. If it had not been for this remnant of men, the Benjaminite Tribe, would have been wipe out for good. The other tribes were saddened the Benjamites had so few men left. They did not want this tribe to be wiped out. To help increase the Benjamites, the other tribes had a solution. They decided to fight against Jabesb Gilead, because they did not assist in the war against the Benjamites.

They killed all the people of Jabesh Gilead, except 400 young women virgins. They took them and gave them to the Benjamites. This began the rebuilding of the Benjamites for the future of the church or twelve tribes They also allowed the Benjamites to take women from Shiloh. The Benjamites took the women of Shiloh against their will, and their parent's will. The Benjamites did not learn a lesson. They repeated the same crime, as they did with the concubine. Obviously, this caused more violence against the women. A familiar sight repeated, as it did with the host of that house. He offered his virgin daughter for the good of man. Here again, another offering or sacrificing of virgins' daughters for the good of man. A little leaven leavens the whole loaf. The Benjamites refused earlier to give up the perverted men so justice would prevail. This left a little leaven to leaven in their lives again. Therefore, they could take women by force or against their will. Evil remained in them from earlier. When we take our focus off God, we risk an absence of the King in our land to lead and guide us into all truth.

An example of no King in Adam and Eve's land

26And God said, Let us make man in our image, after our likeness: and let them have dominion over the fish of the sea, and over the fowl of the air, and over the cattle, and over all the earth, and over every creeping thing that creepeth upon the earth. 27So God created man in his own image, in the image of God created he him; male and female created he them. 28 And God blessed them, and God said unto them, Be fruitful,and multiply, and replenish the earth, and subdue it: and have dominion over the fish of the sea, and over the fowl of the air, and over every living thing that moveth upon the earth. 31 And God saw every thing that he had made and, behold, it was very good. And the evening and the morning were the sixth day.   (Genesis 1:26-28,31) KJV

God created us in His very own image. Man is a copy, double, duplicate and splitting image of God. Everything God is, we are too. God looked at all He created and said it was very good. He saw us excellent in every shape, fashion and form. We are just like God the Father, God the Son and God the Holy Ghost. God gave us authority to rule and reign over what he created, as fish, fowls, livestock, wild animals and whatever crawls on the ground. To reign over something is to have absolute authority, control, rule and influence over it.

15And the Lord God took the man, and put him into the garden of Eden to dress it and to keep it. 16And the Lord God commanded the man, saying, Of every tree of the garden thou mayest freely eat: 17But of the tree of the knowledge of good and evil, thou shalt not eat of it: for in the day that thou eatest thereof thou shalt surely die. 18And the Lord God said, "It is not good that the man should be alone; I will make him an help meet for him".   (Gen, 2:15-18) AKJV

God gave Adam a paradise or the first church. He instructed Adam to attend to the things of God. He had to take care of the supernatural things. He was responsible for the glory, presence and the power of God. All things that happen for Adam were in the supernatural. Therefore, Adam was a supernatural being. He was free in the garden. God did tell him not to eat of the Tree of the Knowledge of Good and Evil; that tree were off limits. God does not want us to have appetite for anything, but the fruit He gives us to partake of. If we eat the wrong thing from the wrong tree, we will die. There are many trees to eat from when there is no King in our land. Those trees will cause death.

Attending church services weekly help in learning what trees to eat from and not eat from. It teaches us there are things beyond our boundaries, which indicates there is no King in the land. God want us to eat the meat of His will, to do the work of the Father which sent us and finish it. Doing His will is our protein and nutrition to live. We also see scripture says God made Adam a wife. This brings us to our next passage of scripture.

1Now the serpent was more subtil than any beast of the field which the Lord God had made. And he said unto the woman, Yea, hath God said, Ye shall not eat of every tree of the garden? 2And the woman said unto the serpent, We may eat of the fruit of the trees of the garden: 3But of the fruit of the tree which is in the midst of the garden, God hath said, Ye shall not eat of it, neither shall ye touch it, lest ye die. 4And the serpent said unto the woman, Ye shall not surely die: 5For God doth know that in the day ye eat thereof, then your eyes shall be opened, and ye shall be as gods, knowing good and evil.

6And when the woman saw that the tree was good for food, and that it was pleasant to the eyes, and a tree to be desired to make one wise, she took of the fruit thereof, and did eat, and gave also unto her husband with her; and he did eat. 7And the eyes of them both were opened, and they knew that they were naked; and they sewed fig leaves together, and made themselves aprons.
(Genesis 3:1-7) KJV

The snake was sneakier than any animals the LORD made. One day the snake went to Eve. His mission was to entice her to become unfocused from the King in her land or life. He asked her if God said not to eat the fruit, from any one of the trees in the garden. She replied, "God allowed them to eat from all the trees, except from the tree in the center of the garden. If they ate or touched the tree, they would die." The snake, the father of lies, lied to her. He told her she would not die and God knew it. And if she did eat the fruit, she would be like God. She would know between right and wrong. Eve had no need to know right and wrong because she and Adam were spiritual. The key is that, Eve was already like God. If she did eat the fruit, she would sin. Therefore, another king, other than God will permeate her life. Eve had a choice to shut down the voice speaking to her. Yet, she chose to continue to entertain the voice that was speaking. It was not the voice of the King, which was in her land or life! The voice of the snake was exalting himself above what Eve knew about God, the true King in her land.

She stared at the beautiful fruit and then ate it. Then she gave it to Adam. Notice when Eve touched the fruit, nothing happened. Notice when Eve tasted it, nothing happened. Notice when her spouse ate the fruit, both of them saw. They saw their nakedness and tried to cover themselves with fig leaves. When the King was once in our land and He is removed; when we listen and obey another voice, we too will try to cover our nakedness.

12th APPROACH

Another Gospel

When we do not see, when we do not hear and when we do not understand spiritual things in our heart, it can become an intruder and a barrier. Spiritual things are spiritually discerned. The natural mind cannot discern these spiritual things, because it follows another gospel. Anything that goes outside of normalcy can become abnormal or perverted.

Galatians 1:6-10 KJV: 6 I marvel that ye are so soon removed from him that called you into the grace of Christ unto another gospel: 7Which is not another; but there be some that trouble you, and would pervert the gospel of Christ. 8But though we, or an angel from heaven, preach any other gospel unto you than that which we have preached unto you, let him be accursed. 9As we said before, so say I now again, if any man preach any other gospel unto you than that ye have received, let him be accursed. 10For do I now persuade men, or God? or do I seek to please men? for if I yet pleased men, I should not be the servant of Christ.

Paul, an apostle of Jesus Christ, has the authority to speak to various issues encountered in the churches. His authority came from God and not men. Paul confronts the Galatians on their eagerness to embrace error. He is counteracting some teachings on salvation. He was shocked over what the Galatians had embraced concerning the Gospel. He called it *Another Gospel*.

ANOTHER GOSPEL IS REALLY NO GOSPEL AT ALL

It is the perverting of the gospel. It is the act of abandoning God for a false gospel. *Another Gospel* is representative of enslavement and serving another master. Hidden motives are not the gospel, but literally a smokescreen. *Another Gospel* was a cover, barrier, influence, authority and blinder to prevent truth from manifesting.

The Galatians were removed from God because they could not see God. When the truth is perverted, it is more difficult to discern than a clear lie. Paul said he was shocked that they were turning away from God. God is the One that called them to be reconciled to Himself through Jesus Christ. They claimed to follow Christ but denied the work He did on the cross; which was sufficient for salvation. They started to follow a different teaching, which seemed to be the Gospel. Should we say this teaching pretended to be the Gospel? But, it is not the Gospel at all.

Many had habitually perverted and distorted the truth to validate what others are to do. This is the reason II Timothy 2:15 states, "We must study the Word of God to show ourselves approved of God, be a workman, need not to be ashamed and rightly dividing the word of truth." If the Word can be rightly divided, it can be wrongly divided. Paul strongly denounced the perverting of the Gospel. He considered twisting the truth of Christ was deliberately fooling them.

Some extreme Jewish Christians were teaching that the Gentiles had to submit to Jewish laws and traditions. They deemed this a necessary addition to believing Christ. Paul had to confront those issues. Jews wanted the believers to follow Jewish laws and customs. He considered this as embracing a different message. It was considered as being alienated, lies, strange, unknown and outlandish. It was a message that was no message at all. It was *Another Gospel*. It was a mixture of law and grace.

The Jews felt faith in Christ was not enough. This teaching undermines the truth that salvation is a gift. Salvation is not a reward for good deeds. Human deeds cannot save us. Salvation is a gift available to all people. These Jewish teachers were called Judaizers because they wanted to turn the Gentiles into Jews. When they set up additional requirements for salvation, they denied the power of Christ' death on the cross. They perverted the Good News because they believed Old Testament practices were required of the new believers. The Gentiles were not familiar with these practices. The Jews and Gentiles both believed in Christ but had different lifestyles. Paul was firm when he said their teaching was perverted and changes the Good News. He wants to ensure nothing perverts the message of Christ, which he preached. Salvation for Jews and Gentiles is by faith in

Christ alone. Believing in Christ is one way and the only way to be forgiven for sin. No other person, method or ritual can give eternal life.

They did not totally deny the foundational truths of the Gospel, but they tried to add to it. They claimed to follow Jesus but denied Jesus' work on the cross was sufficient for salvation. They said, "Jesus is Savior, but salvation is based on your goodness, holiness and performance." They believed that along with Jesus, and doing other rituals, they would be completely saved. Acting well, being good and performing good deeds is not the true Gospel. The Gospel is the Good News or News which is too good to be true. This Good News that is too good to be true, is the Grace of Christ. It is specifically what Jesus did for us. It is based upon His performance, not ours. Our good works and holiness does not earn us salvation. If we can accept the fact by nature we are sinners, we must also accept the fact being born again by nature, we are completely righteous. Righteousness is through Jesus death on the cross. God is only satisfied with the shed blood of Jesus. No other work, performance or sacrifice is needed.

We tend to depend upon ourselves. We promote more trust in self, than promoting our trust in the finished work of the cross. That becomes *Another Gospel*. We believe if we pray daily, try to love everyone, be a good person, read the bible, help others etc., these additional acts complete our salvation. But we are completely save and righteous without them. We have unconsciously and consciously added things to the finished work of Christ. This can become *Another Gospel*. We place demands upon ourselves that are strenuous and grievous. If we fail to live up to the Gospel of performance and expectations, we set up for ourselves to follow; we feel we have failed. This is because we have set up standards that are not required.

Right standing with God is by His grace and not our efforts. Many religions require specific things to be done for us to be acceptable to God. No vast amount of human efforts will make us right with God. Good deeds are good, but they do not give us eternal life. Extra rules and regulation only place burdens upon us, which God did not ordain. Jesus has a much easier yoke for us to take. We cannot save ourselves. When entering God's presence on judgment day, many will say these are my works. "I gave to the poor, was a good person, nice to everyone, never drank alcohol etc." When we do this, we are trusting in our own salvation and what we performed on earth. But as a born-again believer we can stand in God's presence on judgment day. We confess Jesus is Lord and Savior. We will say that we trust in Jesus goodness, Jesus performance, Jesus death, Jesus burial and resurrection.

Galatians 3:1 KJV O foolish Galatians, who hath bewitched you, that ye should not obey the truth, before whose eyes Jesus Christ hath been evidently set forth, crucified among you?

Paul preaching to the Galatians was so clear that he had to ask them, "Who has hypnotized you? Who has placed a spell upon you?" In other words, he was asking them who rendered them stupid, silly, brainless, mindless, unintelligent and unwise. He reminded the Galatians they were acting as though someone had placed a hex upon them. He believed they were so caught up in this false teaching, it was like a magic spell casted upon them. He said this because magic was a common thing in Paul's day. The magicians used both illusions and Satan's power to perform miracles. People were drawn in by their mysterious seduction of sensationalism without discerning or recognizing the source as Satan. Paul was saying it was obvious they no longer focused on the crucifixion of Christ. His teaching made sure Christ's sacrifice on the cross was taught in detail. He encouraged them to trust in Jesus Christ and not the Law. Paul declared in,

Galatians 1:8 KJV: But though we, or an angel from heaven, preach any other gospel unto you, than that which we have preached unto you, let him be accursed.

The law has a curse for those that fail to keep it, and the gospel has a curse for those that seek to change it. The curse is geared toward anyone who preaches anything other than the Gospel Paul preached. Paul extended the curse to include himself, any angel, or persons spreading false teaching. The key to this statement is, if an angel came preaching another message he would not be from heaven. Paul warned in,

14 And no wonder, for even Satan disguises himself as an angel of light. 15 So it is no surprise if his servants, also, disguise themselves as servants of righteousness. Their end will correspond to their deeds.   (II Corinthian 11:14-15) ESV

Satan is a representative of hell

It did not matter how beautiful the angel looked, Satan can parade himself as beautiful light. He is determined to cause things to appear and sound as if it is from God. Paul was so adamant about this paraded deception of Satan; he repeated the statement.

Paul reiterates his words, "As we said before, so say I now again, if any man preaches any other gospel unto you than that ye have received, let him be accursed." The message of the Gospel must never change. Paul considered the perversion of the gospel as a crisis, and a life and death issue. Life and death issues are the crisis of life hanging in the balance. There is a need for CPR, circulation and the rescue breath of Jesus. Paul could speak this way because his message came directly from Christ. He refuses to allow them to spend their lives constantly pleasing others. These new believers deviated from what they knew was correct to please man. Paul declared to them, that he was not trying to please others. He knew no matter what and how much is done for people, it is never enough. His focus was not to become a man pleaser. When a man seeks man's approval, God is left out. This becomes *Another Gospel.* The Apostle Paul said, "If he seeks to please man he could not be a servant of Christ." If he changed his message to please men, he could not be a bondservant of Christ.

He must do everything because of his love for God. Man is only a vessel sent to represent God. If a man pleases God, he will know how to serve as unto the LORD. When men seek to please man, devastation becomes hard to handle if man fails us. Seek God's approval. He is our source above everyone else. We do what we do because we love God.

Matthew 23 reveals an example of *Another Gospel*

It is a barrier, smokescreen, closed heaven, blinders, blockades, authority and influence. It is a perversion of that which is normal. These religious leaders were walking in dangerous territories of landmines. They love positions more than they love God. We see them doing many things unbecoming of a minister. God always warns us through teaching, along with visitations from mighty men and women of God. Jesus visited these leaders to warn them of *Another Gospel.*

1Then spake Jesus to the multitude, and to his disciples, 2Saying the scribes and the Pharisees sit in Moses' seat: 3All therefore whatsoever they bid you observe, that observe and do; but do not ye after their works: for they say, and do not. 4For they bind heavy burdens and grievous to be borne, and lay them on men's shoulders; but they themselves will not move them with one of their fingers. 5But all their works they do for to be seen of men: they make broad their phylacteries, and enlarge the borders of their garments, 6And love the uppermost rooms at feasts, and the chief seats in the synagogues, 7And greetings in the markets, and to be called of men, Rabbi, Rabbi.

8But be not ye called Rabbi: for one is your Master, even Christ; and all ye are brethren. 9And call no man your father upon the earth: for one is your Father, which is in heaven. 10Neither be ye called masters: for one is your Master, even Christ. 11But he that is greatest among you shall be your servant. 12And whosoever shall exalt himself shall be abased; and he that shall humble himself shall be exalted.

13But woe unto you, scribes and Pharisees, hypocrites! for ye shut up the kingdom of heaven against men: for ye neither go in yourselves, neither suffer ye them that are entering to go in. 14Woe unto you, scribes and Pharisees, hypocrites! for ye devour widows' houses, and for a pretense make long prayer: therefore ye shall receive the greater damnation. 15Woe unto you, scribes and Pharisees, hypocrites! for ye compass sea and land to make one proselyte, and when he is made, ye make him twofold more the child of hell than yourselves.

16Woe unto you, ye blind guides, which say, whosoever shall swear by the temple, it is nothing; but whosoever shall swear by the gold of the temple, he is a debtor! 17Ye fools and blind: for whether is greater, the gold, or the temple that sanctifieth the gold? 18And, whosoever shall swear by the altar, it is nothing; but whosoever *sweareth by the gift that is upon it, he is guilty. 19Ye fools and blind: for whether is greater, the gift, or the altar that sanctifieth the gift? 20Whoso therefore shall swear by the altar, sweareth by it, and by all things thereon. 21And whoso shall swear by the temple, sweareth by it, and by him that dwelleth therein. 22And he that shall swear by heaven, sweareth by the throne of God, and by him that sitteth thereon.*

23Woe unto you, scribes and Pharisees, hypocrites! for ye pay tithe of mint and anise and cummin, and have omitted the weightier matters of the law, judgment, mercy, and faith: these ought ye to have done, and not to leave the other undone. 24Ye blind guides, which strain at a gnat, and swallow a camel. 25Woe unto you, scribes and Pharisees, hypocrites! for ye make clean the outside of the cup and of the platter, but within they are full of extortion and excess. 26Thou blind Pharisee, cleanse first that which is within the cup and platter, that the outside of them may be clean also. 27Woe unto you, scribes and Pharisees, hypocrites! for ye are like unto whited sepulchres, which indeed appear beautiful outward, but are within full of dead men's bones, and of all uncleanness. 28Even so ye also outwardly appear righteous unto men, but within ye are full of hypocrisy and iniquity. 29Woe unto you, scribes and Pharisees, hypocrites! because ye build the tombs of the prophets, and garnish the sepulchres of the righteous.
(Matthew 23:1-29) KJV

Jesus addressed the religious leaders as well as his upcoming apostles, church builders and the crowds. He condemned them as hypocrites. The religious leaders considered their application of their tradition, just as important to them as God's law. They believed their man-made rules were equal to God. Jesus gave them accolades in teaching the Word: yet He considered them as frauds and deceivers. They are good with the Law of Moses, but the people are to beware of following their example. They were not practicing what they taught. They knew the Word but exhibited no change in their lives. They testified to following Jesus, but they did not live by Jesus standard of love. Their actions needed to follow the Word of God. They talk a good talk but did not walk any of it out. They wore a well-painted, colorful detailed mask called hypocrisy. They took God's Word and created rules that burdened the people. They loved to see the people staggering under these loads. They never reached out to give the people a hand. Many things they did were for show. They loved to look holy to receive praise and admiration. They loved to sit in areas to be seen and flattered in words of honor and praises about their degrees.

Instead of leading people, they were blind guides. They gag when swallowing a gnat but swallowed a camel with no problem. In other words, they knit pick over small things, but ignore the large things involving the Word and people. They gave, but not to the widows, an area that really needed addressing. They washed areas of their lives that were visible to others. Yet, their heart was greedy, selfish and dirty. They did not represent what they displayed outwardly. Another description Jesus gave was; they were like a tomb washed outside, but their insides were like dead men bones. They were useless, because the inside and outside lifestyle did not lineup. On the outside they look good, but the inside was evil. They pretended to be good. They had a form of godliness, but they denied the power thereof. Their lives were considered roadblocks or *Another Gospel*. In *Another Gospel* they were preventing people from going to heaven, and they themselves will not go either.

Let us look at the culture which is *Another Gospel* in Isaiah 6

Barriers and cultures blocked the king's focus on God. He became slack in his obedience to God. Culture is what we do. Culture, in a negative way can destroy purpose when we know to do right and still do wrong. It becomes *Another Gospel*. Remember, the Galatians were taught the Word of God. They knew what to do. They were taught well by Apostle Paul, but the culture of the extreme Jews, penetrated their lives. The culture was an abnormality that threatened the normal. Culture can be the counterfeit, which can apprehend the genuine. Negative culture was symbolic of *Another Gospel*. It caused the Galatians to become mesmerized, hypnotized and they soon pulled away from the Gospel of Jesus Christ.

1 In the year that king Uzziah died I saw also the Lord sitting upon a throne, high and lifted up, and his train filled the temple. 2 Above it stood the seraphims: each one had six wings; with twain he covered his face, and with twain he covered his feet, and with twain he did fly. 3 And one cried unto another, and said,

Holy, holy, holy, is the Lord of hosts: the whole earth is full of his glory.   *(Isaiah 6:1-3) KJV*

King Uzziah became king at age sixteen and reigned fifty-two years. He had opportunity to become a great king. During his early years as king, he was quite successful as ruler. God allowed him to become prosperous. Also, God warned the Israelites during that time including the prophets, priests and king, not to become proud of their prosperity. This was according to Deuteronomy 30:17-20. God said,

17But if thine heart turn away, so that thou wilt not hear, but shalt be drawn away, and worship other gods, and serve them; 18I denounce unto you this day, that ye shall surely perish, and that ye shall not prolong your days upon the land, whither thou passest over Jordan to go to possess it. 19 I call heaven and earth to record this day against you, that I have set before you life and death, blessing and cursing: therefore choose life, that both thou and thy seed may live: 20That thou mayest love the LORD thy God, and that thou mayest obey his voice, and that thou mayest cleave unto him: for he is thy life, and the length of thy days: that thou mayest dwell in the land which the LORD sware unto thy fathers, to Abraham, to Isaac, and to Jacob, to give them.
                                (Deuteronomy 30:17-20) KJV

King Uzziah apparently forgot the warnings of Moses and the prophets. The LORD had helped Uzziah in all his achievements, but King Uzziah became proud of his power. This led to his downfall. II Chronicles 26:16-22 explains; one day King Uzziah disobeyed God by going into the temple. He proceeded burning incense as an offering to God. Azariah, the priest and eighty other brave priests followed Uzziah into the temple. They said, "Your Majesty, this isn't right. You are not allowed to burn incense to the LORD. This is to be done only by priests who are descendants of Aaron. You will have to leave. You have sinned against the LORD. Therefore, He will no longer bless you. We take our hands off what God is not blessing".

Uzziah was standing next to the incense altar at the time. He held the incense burner, ready to offer incense to the LORD. He became very angry when he heard Azariah's warning. Leprosy suddenly developed upon his forehead. Azariah and the other priests saw it and immediately told him to leave the temple. Uzziah realized that the LORD had punished him, and he hurried to go outside. Uzziah suffered from that moment forward with leprosy for the rest of his life. He no longer was allowed in the temple or in his own palace. Leprosy prevented Uzziah from burial in the royal tombs. Instead, he was buried in a nearby cemetery the kings owned. His son, Jotham ruled in his place. Prophet Isaiah, son of Amoz, write about everything Uzziah did as king.

God assigned certain responsibilities to the priests. No king could usurp the authority and duties of the priests. When we are blessed, we must not become prideful in our accomplishments. The fall of Uzziah was directly related to his heart becoming proud. He felt he could move beyond his measure of authority. Many other people fell away from God as well. This is proof that we cannot move beyond our measure of authority. We need authority for what we do for God. The priests of the Mosaic covenant were authorized to offer sacrifices. They were authorized to burn incense on the altar of incense. Neither prophets nor king had that authority. Something similar happened to Nadab and Abihu.

1 And Nadab and Abihu, the sons of Aaron, took either of them his censer, and put fire therein, and put incense thereon, and offered strange fire before the LORD, which he commanded them not. 2 And there went out fire from the LORD, and devoured them, and they died before the LORD.   (Leviticus 10: 1-2) KJV

God means what he says. Notice how this king left God's Authority and moved into *Another Gospel*. The king's vision is always set before the people. Whatever is the king's vision, becomes the culture of the people. The king has authority and power in his words. Whatever he legislates is legislated in the land. Where the Word of the king is, there is power. The king set up rules and regulations for the people to follow. He has influence. He speaks words into the lives of the people. He is the example and pattern set before the people by God. His voice rules the lives of his subjects. He dictates the custom and manners to the people.

Once upon a time this king was a good king. He had a long prosperous reign, but his heart became proud. If a king or a person in authority never move in pride, he will not have a problem trying to come down. This king also served without an order from God. It is dangerous when we do not follow the plan of God, because we set up our own plans. He moved into a position in ministry God had not ordained. He moved beyond his measure of authority. He was trying to offer strange fires to God. Therefore, he moved into a form of godliness, but denied the power thereof. When the ruler becomes unruly there is no vision for the people. Therefore, the people perish or fall away from God. The people will cast off restraints or the harness of God.

In summary, King Uzziah left God's way and set up his own rules. He made a decision on how he would follow God. It was his human effort. It was his performance. It was his desire. He left what he knew and moved out of the position of being a king. He went into another area and served without an order from God. He added his ingredients to what God had decreed for the temple. He added himself into the priesthood. When he did this, he added *Another Gospel*. He moved out of position, to produce something God did not ordain. He was not focused.

In the year that king Uzziah died I saw also the Lord sitting upon a throne, high and lifted up, and his train filled the temple.
(Isaiah 6:1) KJV

In other words, the earthly king was dead, but Isiah saw the spiritual king. The earthly king Uzziah is symbolic of habits, barriers, intrusions, blinders, strongholds, bondages, cover-up, illnesses, unforgiveness, pornography, divisions, veils, rejection, fornication, adultery, gossip, backbiting, murmuring, complaining, anger, deception, lust, money, smokescreen, addictions, money, lust, rebellion or strongholds that prevents us from seeing, hearing or understanding God. These things become *Another Gospel*.

Heaven was not accessible to Isaiah until king Uzziah died. He could not see before that. The earthly king did not have keen spiritual eyesight, neither insight into God's destiny and purpose for the people. He had no vision. He was in darkness concerning a vast number of things. Whatever is in the dark will come or submit to the light. Therefore, darkness kept Isaiah earthbound. Jesus died so we can see. He does not want us in bondage or bound by earthly things, laws and rules. We are heavenly citizens governed by heaven regulations and laws.

King Uzziah had to die so Isaiah could hear, see and understand God for himself. It was really time for Isaiah to see spiritually. Isaiah said, "During the year the king died, he also saw the LORD." He saw for himself in a personal way, the Father, the Son and Holy Spirit. All three persons appeared in this vision. He saw with eyes of the understanding, in the vision of prophecy. He saw Christ as Lord.

Two events happened in one year, both impacted Isaiah

These events are related to: *The LORD he saw*. And God showed Isaiah death and life. Both will be fulfilled in the ONE he saw sitting on the throne; Christ. The death of the earthly king on the throne, which is Uzziah, and the life of the heavenly King on the throne, which is Jesus Christ, was seen. Next, Jesus conquerors death forever and replaces it with eternal life through Himself. Jesus is the King that gives life.

When Isaiah saw the LORD, it became his access into the spiritual and heavenly realm. The veil or covers were peeled back so Isaiah could get a glimpse. Whenever God peels back the heavens, it is because He gives us important revelations. He is going to visit and do something for us. Therefore, He wants us in position. He will declare, we are His beloved sons in whom He is well pleased. God wanted to show Isaiah how the earthly kingdom is supposed to be, according to His Heavenly Kingdom. For Isaiah to receive a Word of the LORD, the king Uzziah had to die in Isaiah's life. When the king died, relationships died. The king's death represents all authority or relationships that prevents him from seeing God clearly.

When the king's death occurred, and the relationship was over, it was the only time Isaiah could move. As soon as the king died, Isaiah heard the voice of God. As soon as the king died, Isaiah talked with God. As soon as the king died, Isaiah saw into the Spirit realm. As soon as the king died, Isaiah understood his call, mission, directions, source and spiritual assignment. As soon as the king died, Isaiah saw a true king. When we declare the king is dead in our lives, we began to live.

Kings come, and kings go, but the new King Isaiah saw spiritually a kingdom with no end; Jesus. Uzziah earthly kingdom ended. Jesus Himself is the One, who is high and exalted above all creatures. Jesus is high and lifted, not His throne. Everyone and everything is under Him and submits to His authority. The glory of the Lord filled heaven and earth. After Jesus humiliation here on earth, we behold Him crowned with glory and honor. His reign is forever. He was reigning in glory and majesty. It was the risen Christ; the heart for the gospel. He is the King of kings and Lord of lords. Heaven is His throne and earth is His footstool. He is seated far above all principalities, rulers, powers and spiritual wickedness in high places.

Our body is the temple of the Lord. The LORD's train, hem or presence reached here on earth. The train is the skirts, borders or lower parts of the garments, reaching earth, just to fill Isaiah's temple for service. You shall receive power after the Holy Ghost comes upon you (or train fills your temple), and ye shall become a witness unto Me. On the day of Pentecost, suddenly there was a sound from heaven as of a rushing mighty wind and it filled the temple. God's representative must be filled with the Holy Spirit.

Above it stood the seraphim's: each one had six wings; with twain he covered his face, and with twain he covered his feet, and with

twain he did fly. 3 And one cried unto another, and said, Holy, holy, holy, is the Lord of hosts: the whole earth is full of his glory.
(Isaiah 6:2-3) KJV

Isaiah is seeing from a heavenly perspective now. The smokescreen of another gospel was removed and dead. He sees the glory of the heavenly King. In the past he saw an earthly king with man's glory. He sees something he never saw before. The seraphim are symbolic of the life of Isaiah when he starts moving in ministry. God went further into this vision. He showed Isaiah how God's ministry is to run in earth. God used the seraphim as demonstrators for Isaiah. They were attending and focusing on the LORD on the right hand and on the left hand. They stood as servants ready to wait upon Him. They were ready to receive from Him. They enjoyed communion with Him. They were serving the LORD. They sought approval from God to please Him.

The name seraphim, signifies "burning". Ezekiel's living creatures are said to be like burning coals of fire. Ministers of the Gospel are called ministers of flaming fire as well. It is because of spiritual gifting; carrying and delivery of God's Word. Its effectiveness is compared to fire and the Spirit of God. The apostles had this bestowed on them. They were baptized with the Holy Spirit and with fire. These are the angels of fire. Isaiah is to become a minster of flaming fire, for the work he is called to.

Isaiah noticed how the seraphim were attending to Him. They used their body parts to minister, as Isaiah will use his body parts to minister. The minister that attends to the work of the LORD must do it with their body. The angels covered their face in humility; they saw themselves as less than the least of all the saints. They consider themselves as the chief of sinners. They were not able to look upon the His brilliance, beauty and glory. They were conscious of their sinfulness and unworthiness in His presence. These angels always beheld the face of God.

The Word of God used words beginning with the letter "F" to minister to the LORD - their FACE, FEET and FLY. We will use the "F" in ministry. When we minister to God's people we are ministering to the LORD. The "F's" symbolizes body part ministry. Their body is symbolic of the body ministry in the church.

(A) FACE-they are prostrating on their face, in God's face, to be able to face the people; because their countenance will be from His face so they will not be afraid or worry about the people's face.

(B) FEET- their feet are beautiful that preach the gospel.

He must use his feet to cover worldwide territory. Feet are symbolic of his walk with people and his walk with God. Feet means there are places we will just have to shake the dust off our feet. His feet will be like hind feet. Feet are symbolic of walking in the spirit and not fulfilling the lust of his flesh.

(C) FLY is the speed they will go into the spirit and spiritual things. Fly is the sailing through every aspect of ministry with ease. Fly is the continuous navigation in the spiritual gifts, power, authority, anointing and the word of God. Fly means they are not subject to time and space because they are eternal spirit beings. Fly means God is going to hasten His word to perform it for them. Fly means God is going to escalate and redeem lost time.

Even in the public ministry, our voice is to cry holy, holy and holy. All of this indicates how the public ministry of the seraphim was in harmony and unity. We as ministers are in the public eye. We must be in harmony and unity at all times. Everything in ministry is done in decency and order. There should be no division in ministry. God shows up in unity. The seraphim's answered one another and agreed in what they said. They even agreed on the holiness of God, the Son and the Spirit. All three were glorious in holiness. There is glory in the Holy Father, and the Holy Son, and the Holy Ghost. His glory covers the earth, as the water covers the sea, as if He was still in the earth.

4And the posts of the door moved at the voice of him that cried, and the house was filled with smoke. 5Then said I, Woe is me! <u>for I am undone</u>; because I am a man of unclean lips, and I dwell in the midst of a people of unclean lips: for mine eyes have seen the King, the Lord of hosts. 6Then flew one of the seraphims unto me, having a live coal in his hand, which he had taken with the tongs from off the altar: 7And he laid it upon my mouth, and said, Lo, *this hath touched thy lips; and thine iniquity is taken away, and thy sin purged.* (Isaiah 6:4-7) KJV

This is the presence of God in His church with the ministers moving in signs, miracles and wonders. We as the many member Body of Christ will be waiting upon or serving the Lord. This is done as we go out to preach the gospel to the poor, open blind eyes, set the captives free, raise the dead and heal the sick. When we do it for the least of these we have done it for the LORD. Even the pillars of the church tremble at God's voice, as He uses His ministers.

Isaiah saw the LORD and heard the voices of the angels praising. He realized how sinful he was. He says, "Woe is me". Jesus said the same woe when he spoke to the religious leaders in Matthew 23. This indicates the behavior of a person as grievous to Jesus. Isaiah sees his behavior as grievous to God. He was also surrounded by a culture of wicked men. Therefore, he saw himself as he saw them. He says he is undone. He feels undone because he had been quiet in ministry. He may have performed his duty in the past; yet not in the full capacity that he was ordained, while in his mother's womb. Isaiah never says his heart or works were unclean. He says his lips are unclean. It was his lips that caused him to sin. He sinned because he never moved out into being that voice or minister into the greater anointing as a prophet. He sinned by not speaking the words of God to full capacity out of his mouth. This made him uneasy. He felt it was over.

He felt he was doomed because of sin life. He soon realizes his lips were filthy. The Jewish people around him were filthy as well. They taught doctrines of men which opposed and blasphemed the truths of the Gospel; *Another Gospel*. Living among men of filthy speech and conversation is a concern to him. It troubled the spirit. This man was in danger of learning their words. He was in danger of suffering from being in their culture. When Isaiah lips were touch with a coal of fire, God said, he was forgiven. It was God that cleanse him and not the coals.

8Also I heard the voice of the Lord, saying, Whom shall I send, and who will go for us? Then said I, Here am I; send me. 9And he said, Go, and tell this people, Hear ye indeed, but understand not; and see ye indeed, but perceive not. 10Make the heart of this people fat, and make their ears heavy, and shut their eyes; lest they see with their eyes, and hear with their ears, and understand with their heart, and convert, and be healed. (Isaiah 6:8-10) KJV

This is God promoting the prophet's ministry. His iniquity was taken, and God forgave him. *Another Gospel* that prevented Isaiah from full capacity of the prophetic ministry is now over. The prophet was free to go and freely minister for the LORD. He had no barriers, blockage, bondage, influences etc. that would prevent him from writing and speaking for God. Isaiah was an active prophet during the reign of five kings. By the time Uzziah died God had established Isaiah as a scribe in the royal palace in Jerusalem. He had a nice prophetic career.

He was commissioned to speak and write messages for people that would not listen.

GOD NEVER TOLD ISAIAH THE OFFICE WOULD BE EASY

He never said he would have great success, but eventually people would listen. The bible says, "Whom shall I send to prophesy and who will go teach them." Isaiah is the one that said, "Send Me Lord, I Will Go!" The LORD knew whom to send. He knew he would be the LORD's voice. He will be the Word to the people of Israel. This was the same one that was undone and felt unworthy to be in the service of God. He answered the call. He was told to go tell this people that preached *Another Gospel* what their condition is. Reprove them for their blindness.

This is the new direction of the calling of Isaiah the prophet. This is the advanced anointing to prophesy. It is the purpose of the vision. It is the purpose of the calling. Go preach the judgment of God so they can change, be converted and healed. Not hearing, not seeing and not being able to understand spiritual things is considered a closed heaven, barrier, stronghold, authority, influence, intruder or smoke screen. The spiritual things are spiritually discerned. The natural mind cannot spiritually discern this because it follows *Another Gospel*.

God wanted the Jews to become focused on Him. He sends the prophet to them because they are rebellious.

God knew they would hear the prophet but not learn from his message. Their hearts were stony and beyond repentance. God had become impatience with them and decides to abandon them to their hard hearts. God's conclusion; if we couldn't see with eyes spiritually, we are sick. If we cannot hear with ears spiritually, we are sick. If we do not understand with our heart spiritually, we are sick. God assumes we are sick and need healing, if we cannot see, hear and understand spiritually. He said at any time we are converted, change our mind and remove ourselves from *Another Gospel,* we can be converted, and He will heal us. Without a shadow of a doubt, we will be healed. Isaiah 6:8-10 and Matthew 13:13-17 says the same.

8Then I heard the voice of the Lord saying, 'Whom shall I send, and who will go for us?' And I said, 'Here am I; send me!' 9And he said, 'Go and say to this people: "Keep listening, but do not comprehend; keep looking, but do not understand." 10Make the mind of this people dull, and stop their ears, and shut their eyes, so that they may not look with their eyes, and listen with their ears, and comprehend with their minds, and turn and be healed.'
(Isaiah 6:8-10) AKJV

13Therefore speak I to them in parables: because they seeing see not; and hearing they hear not, neither do they understand. 14And in them is fulfilled the prophecy of Esaias, which saith, By hearing ye shall hear, and shall not understand; and seeing ye shall see, and shall not perceive: 15For this people's heart is waxed gross, and their ears are dull of hearing, and their eyes they have closed; lest at any time they should see with their eyes and hear with their ears, and should understand with their heart, and should be converted, and I should heal them. 16But blessed are your eyes, for they see: and your ears, for they hear. 17For verily I say unto you, that many prophets and righteous men have desired to see those things which ye see and have not seen them; and to hear those things which ye hear, and have not heard them.   *(Matthew 13:13-17) KJV*

Conclusion

Now that you have read this book, you have come to identify and understand the treasure of deep mysteries within you. God is piercing your world with wealth, knowledge and confirmation about your encounter with Him. If you are relentlessly in seeking the truth, *The Prophetic Approach to FOCUS* will continue to guide you in retention of that prophetic focus.

No longer will you thirst for earthly satisfaction or earthly water. When you drink natural water to quench your thirst, satisfaction is temporary. You become thirsty again as the truth reveals in John 4 about the Samaritan woman's insatiable thirst. You too can get rid of your thirst once and for all. You will no longer thirst from loneliness, rejection, insecurity, lack of love, etc. You are on a pathway that leads you to the Living Water, which is Jesus. No longer will you go from relationship to relationship and remain thirsty. After choosing to drink Jesus' Living Water, you will never thirst again.

Allow God to continue to unveil the vast amounts of mysteries waiting to be unearthed from the Word of God. Continue to share these as well as your own revealed mysteries from God to the world.

Thank you for going on this journey of the twelve prophetic approaches of focus. I pray that you will allow your heart to be drawn to exploring the mysteries presented in this book from His Word.

13 Therefore speak I to them in parables: because they seeing see not; and hearing they hear not, neither do they understand. 14 And in them is fulfilled the prophecy of Esaias, which saith, By hearing ye shall hear, and shall not understand; and seeing ye shall see, and shall not perceive: 15For this people's heart is waxed gross, and their ears are dull of hearing, and their eyes they have closed; lest at any time they should see with their eyes and hear with their ears, and should understand with their heart, and should be converted, and I should heal them. 16But blessed are your eyes, for they see: and your ears, for they hear. 17For verily I say unto you, that many prophets and righteous men have desired to see those things which ye see and have not seen them; and to hear those things which ye hear, and have not heard them. (Matthew 13:13-17) KJV

ABOUT THE AUTHOR

Dr. Margaret H. Moore

Dr. Margaret H. Moore shares her prophetic view in *The Prophetic Approach to FOCUS*. Her approach is to teach the Word of God in a holistic manner. She believes that a person's total being is important to God. Therefore, knowing and understanding the Word of God is Imperative.

Her love and dedication to God have caused her to live by the motto that, "Whatever is important to God is important to her".

She is called into the prophetic, and currently pastors with her husband, Apostle Melvin E. Moore at Kingdom Connection Ministries International, located in Fayetteville, North Carolina.

She is the mother of three wonderful daughters; has five grandchildren and two great-grandchildren.

Let's Keep in Touch

For more information about the ministry of Dr. Margaret H. Moore and available messages, speaking engagements, spiritual growth and development resources; you may contact:

Kingdom Connection Ministries International
1729 McArthur Road
Fayetteville North Carolina 28311

Phone: (910) 764-1532
Email: mm1moore@aol.com
Website: kingdomconnectionministries.org

References

Life Application Bible; New Living Translation, Second Edition. Red Letter Edition. Tyndale House Publishers, Inc. Carol Steam, Illinois. Copyright 2007.

King James Study Bible. Holman Bible Publishers. Nashville, Tennessee. Copyright 2012.

Matthew Henry's Commentary. Zondervan's Classic Reference Series, In One Volume. Copyright 1961.

William MacDonald. Thomas Nelson Publishers. Believer's Bible Commentary, A Complete Bible Commentary in One. Copyright 1995.

Warren W. Wiebe. Thomas Nelson Publishers. Nashville, TN. Nelson's Quick Reference, Chapter by Chapter Bible Commentary. Copyright 1991.

Eugene H. Peterson. The Message. The Bible in Contemporary Language. Navpress. Copyright 2002.

Zondervan. Today's Parallel Bible. NIV. NASB. KJV. NLT. Copyright 2000.

Roy Allen, H. Wayne House and Earl Radmacher. Thomas Nelson, Inc., Publishers. Nashville, TN. Compact Bible Commentary. 2004.

H. D. M. Spence and Joseph S. Exell. The Pulpit Commentary. Volumes 1-23. Hendrickson Publishers. Peabody, Massachusetts.

Leong M, Phillips LG. Wound healing. In: Townsend CM, Beauchamp RD, Evers BM, Mattox KL, eds. Sabiston Textbook of Surgery: The Biological Basis of Modern

Surgical Practice. 20th ed. Philadelphia, PA: Elsevier; 2017: chap 6. Perry AG, Potter PA, Ostendorf V. Wound care and irrigations. In: Perry AG, Potter PA, Ostendorf V, eds.

Clinical Nursing Skills and Techniques. 8th ed. Philadelphia, PA: Elsevier Mosby; 2014: chapter 38.
Review Date 5/24/2016-Updated by: Mary C. Mancini, MD, PhD, Department of Surgery, Louisiana State University Health Sciences Center, Shreveport, LA. Review provided by VeriMed Healthcare Network. Also reviewed by David Zieve, MD, MHA, Isla Ogilvie, PhD, and the A.D.A.M. Editorial team.

Stress Symptoms, Signs, and Causes; Help guide. Org. Authors: Jeanne Segal, Ph.D., Melinda Smith, M.A., Robert Segal, M.A., and Lawrence Robinson. Last updated: February 2017.

USDA Forest Service, Fire & Aviation Management
3833 S. Development Ave. Boise, ID 83705.

There is A Call in The Land to Focus, Melvin E Moore. Copyright 2016.

Strongman's His Name, What's his game? An Authoritative Biblical Approach to Spiritual Warfare, Dr. Jerry and Carol Roberson. Whitaker House. Baldwin Park, CA. Copyright 1954.

RX -Jesus Wants You Well, C.S. Lovett, MA., B.D., D.D. Personal Christianity. Copyright 1973.

Grace to Give, Apostle Tony Brazelton, VCMI. Suitland Maryland. Copyright 2015.

Bible Gateway, Biblegateway.com.

NOTES

NOTES

NOTES

NOTES

www.ingramcontent.com/pod-product-compliance
Lightning Source LLC
LaVergne TN
LVHW041612070426
835507LV00008B/196